Seven Steps to Heaven

Sailing the Atlantic

Brian Thomas

To Pat
And many adventures with you sailing.
Brian Thomas 16/12/12

All rights reserved. No part of this publication may be reproduced in any form or by any means - graphic, electronic or mechanical, including photocopying, recording, taping or information storage and retrieval systems – without the prior permission in writing of the publishers.

Copyright © 2011 Brian Thomas

ISBN   978-1-4476-3617-5

Acknowledgement

To my wife Diane for her unending patience, support, and understanding

&

Barbara and Pam (Snickers) for their unstinting work checking my very poor grasp of English

Abbreviations & Nicknames

DwW   Dances with Waves

WCC   World Cruising Club

SYC   Sussex Yacht Club

SSB   Single Sideband

Larry   The Autohelm

Doris   The Duogen

Ernie   The Engine

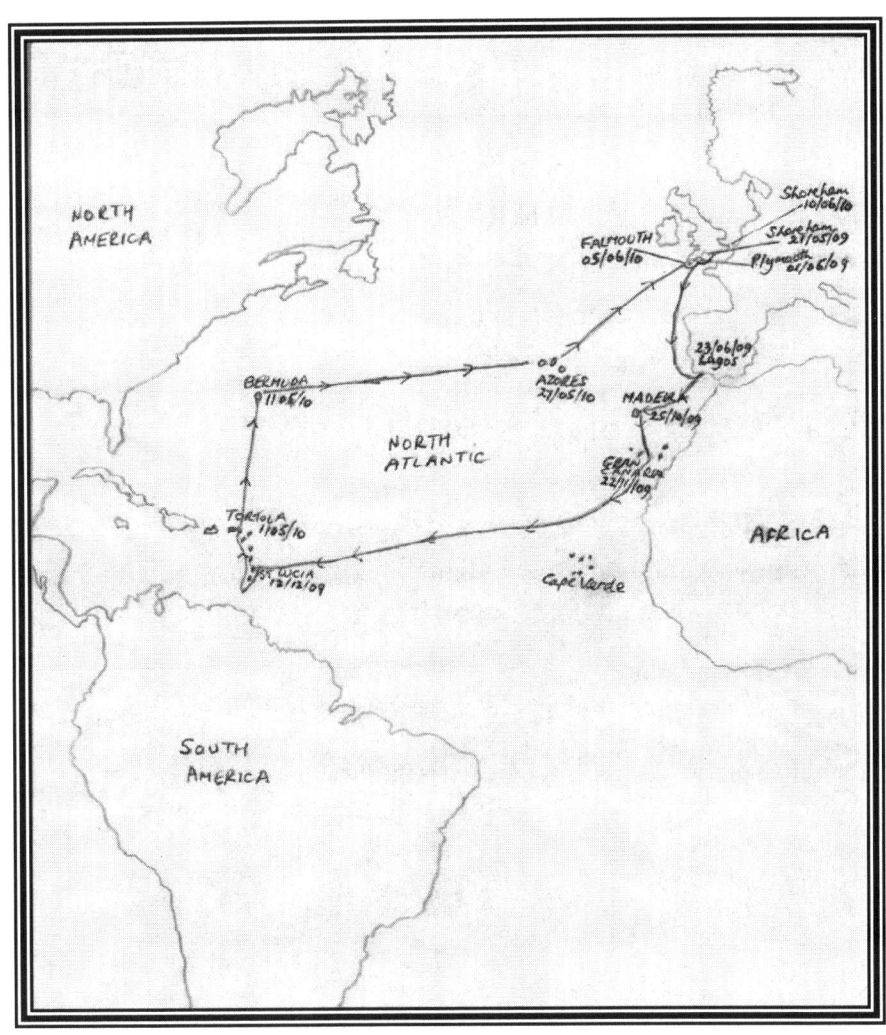

CONTENTS

Foreword	07
First Step to Heaven -Lets choose a Boat	22
Second Step to Heaven -We leave Shoreham for Plymouth	81
Third Step to Heaven – Portugal Rally	85
Fourth Step to Heaven – Off to The Canaries	141
Fifth Step to Heaven – Crossing the Atlantic	154
Sixth Step to Heaven - Touring the Caribbean	177
Seventh Step to Heaven – Back across the Atlantic and Home	243

COVER IMAGE	09
Hard day at the office, Jumby Bay, Antigua	
IMAGE 2	45
The Royal Escape, Fecamp	
IMAGE 3	81
Dances with Waves starts her adventure from Shoreham Lock	
IMAGE 4	107
Notorious Alvor, Portugal	
IMAGE 5	140
Whale or optical illusion?	
IMAGE 6	154
First over the line, Gran Canaria	
IMAGE 7	182
Heaven or Paradise? Palm island, The Grenadines	
IMAGE 8	243
Jome Marina, Road Town, Tortola	

Foreword

This is a story about a person who wanted to complete a dream that had transpired over a lifetime in which normal stages of one's time on this earth were to unfold. Stages such as growing up through teenage years, starting to build a career, meeting a girl, getting married, having a family and retiring.

I am one of the fortunate members of the war babies era. We experienced a completely different lifestyle than our parents and forbearers. It was a time of energy growth and unlimited opportunities. My path enabled me to retire with just enough capital to plan my lifelong dream to sail the Atlantic. The reader will quickly realise that I started this adventure with a large helping of blissful ignorance. Perhaps that was not a bad thing bearing in mind what I was taking on.

My sailing experience was very limited. What you might call a weekend sailor. My parents never had the sailing bug, but I don't think it ever passed a moment's thought for my father, even if he did posses the finances to do such a thing. I was alone in my enthusiasm for sailing amongst my 3 other brothers and many friends and associates. So I am at a loss to comprehend why it was such a bee in my bonnet.

What is even more remarkable is the way we all start something and being human feel obliged to finish. It doesn't occur to us to stop and consider what we are really taking on.

It's like the snowball rolling down the hill. Once momentum is started there is no stopping the forward rush until the bottom is reached. I'm glad my snowball never deviated or broke up or hit a brick wall on the way down. However there were many moments when it very nearly run out of steam and met meltdown. Here is my story in all its raw and open honesty.

First Step to Heaven -Let's choose a Boat
Second Step to Heaven -We leave Shoreham for Plymouth
Third Step to Heaven – Portugal Rally
Fourth Step to Heaven – Off to The Canaries
Fifth Step to Heaven – Crossing the Atlantic
Sixth Step to Heaven - Touring the Caribbean
Seventh Step to Heaven – Back across the Atlantic and Home

Hard day at the office – Jumby Beach, Antigua

A Dream is Born

It all started back in 1976. At the time I was working for ITT Business systems as an Account manager which in layman's terms is another word for salesman.

Diane (my wife) and I had moved from a job in London to Nottingham and now I was responsible for an area covering Yorkshire to Northumberland. You may ask why I had to travel 30 miles north before I was on my patch but that was how it was in the early computer pioneering days. One day I was visiting a company near Skegness. It was a lovely summer's day with blue skies. The wind was light. This is not the usual combination for the east coast but today was the perfect day.

I made my call to a local firm and then decided it would be nice to see Skegness and the sea.

I parked my car and made my way to the promenade and there below me was Scunthorpe Marina. Nothing special I thought, until I glanced to my left and saw a yacht leaving the marina with a man on the wheel (presumably the skipper/owner) and 4 bikini clad girls laid out on the foredeck.

I couldn't help but wonder how some middle aged guy could afford such a wonderful boat and attract 4 lovely young girls. Where else could one manage to do this? My instant reaction was I want some of this and how I can do likewise.

At the time I was living in Nottingham. I was 32 and Diane had just delivered our first son Matthew. The economy was recovering from the effects of the electricity and coal miners' actions and business was not exactly great.

My first boat

So my dream of sailing into the sunset with 4 lovely girls on board my boat would have to be put on hold. However, not to be deterred a friend of the family gave me a wooden tender with a mast and sail so I set about renovating it. After a few months it looked beautiful. Shiny varnished wood and bright new paint.

We decided it would be nice to show off our "boat" the next time I visited the family back down south. So off we set with the dinghy and trailer to Warlingham in Surrey.

During the weekend we took everyone down to Wyre Mill Lake. I launched the boat, successfully hoisted the sail and set off. About 200 yards out I swung the rudder over to return and suddenly saw the rudder fall off. Whoops I had no steering and no oars. The rudder pinion screws had dislodged and fallen off the bracket. Yes it does help to check standing and running gear. My embarrassment was clear to see. Luckily another dinghy towed me to a reception of laughs and guffaws from one and all.

I parked the dinghy and trailer in the yard and a couple of months later sold it for the princely sum of £75. The trailer itself had cost me £150 so add on renovation material costs and I was much lighter in the pockets. Of course later in life I was to realise that sailing is a continuous shower of lost pound notes.

This was a far cry from the beautiful Skegness vision.

More escapades

The dream to own a boat large enough for a crew especially bikini clad lovelies with the accompanying baggage was very much on hold. Also the family and job really put the mockers on any ideas of sailing off into the horizon so it was a question of head down and family fun.

My next opportunity came when I was awarded a sales quota trip to Greece. We stayed in a rather plush hotel with sports activities including sailing dinghies. I believe the model was an Olympic 470. A colleague who was well into laser racing suggested we go for a sail. I jumped at the offer. So off we went. About one mile out the wind began to build substantially and on the next tack we flipped over. No problem I thought, but then the hull felt very heavy and we couldn't right the boat. Eventually after approx 30 minutes it come up and flipped straight over on the opposite side. The wind was getting stronger and the clouds darker. I was feeling very tired.

We were beginning to think something was amiss. The yacht boathouse should have seen us or perhaps wondered why we had not returned as our time was up. Then a catamaran appeared from behind. It didn't take any explaining especially as he didn't speak any English. He threw a line across and we soon arrived back on shore, discovering the hull split and half full of water. No wonder we couldn't right the thing

We never did see the boathouse attendant again.

The hotel management were very understanding and apologetic.

Luckily I was not fazed by this introduction to sailing, never occurring to me how these two incidents could have developed into more serious affairs. I just remember the adrenaline rush and the after burn excitement, as my future adventures will show.

Whitbread Race

By the early nineties my sailing experiences were still limited to the occasional sail in a dinghy, so proper sailing in a yacht and all that it entailed were not apparent. Then a colleague from work lent me a video of the Whitbread race called 'Competing around the world'.

The image of a boat surfing down 20 foot waves in the Southern Ocean at 20 knots was unbelievably vivid. It was where I wanted to be. Then I enquired about cost - £26,000 for the whole trip and around £6000 for the southern ocean. Not a sum I could get near too and also apart from getting the time off work. But the dream still remained.

It was at this time that my colleague who was a keen yachtsman organised a yearly Cowes event in aid of 'sail for cancer'. He chartered the complete Sunsail fleet and organised daily races alongside the main Cowes regatta. It was a tremendous success and taught me a lot about yachts and sailing. But as any sailor will realise it takes a lot more than a days sail to even start understanding how a yacht performs. It's a combination of a house, caravan, airplane, car and whole universe apart from dinghy sailing. My sailing experience was still minimal.

Strangely enough it was my first favourite sport that really converted me to sailing and the sea. Since 1976 I had played golf to a handicap of 11 and travelled to Spain, Scotland and Ireland. I was obsessed about my abilities and one day during a tour with my brothers I hit an iron off the tee and it went sideways. This was a very bad day for me. I quit the tour and returned home by train. I was very sad. This so affected my confidence that every time I went to play I was scared stiff of hitting an iron. They call this disease 'shanking' and normally it is very minimal, but not me. I even tried using a five and seven wood but then my pitching wedge caught the 'disease'. I went to a physiologist who played soothing music and spoke of dwelling on the positive side of golf such as a nice pint in the clubhouse rather than shanking all around the golf course. I later worked out that it wasn't the shanks but a complete cop out as when I swung the club back towards the ball, I was quitting through sheer terror of hitting the ball sideways.

I came to the conclusion that all the years of enjoyable golf in beautiful places were coming to an end and I should concentrate on my original Skegness dream. But it was sometime before it all came together.

Money was always a challenge and although the golf left me extra free time to concentrate on something else, the cost of a yacht was still prohibitive.

Of course on reflection I could have bought a small boat to begin with, but it never really crossed my mind, especially as I had plenty of other priorities to occupy my spare time. Employing workmen for DIY jobs was never an option and so decorating, gardening, car repairs and time with the family were more than enough to take up the free weekends and holidays.

We were very happy living in Nottingham were we had our first son and then from 1977 we moved to Cheshire again because of the job and continued to grow the family with the addition of Jamie and lastly Cara our daughter.

Cancer scare

The next five years proved to be the most happy and most dreadful in my life. The slower village life of Cheshire was in complete contrast to the stress of travelling and working for a demanding sales organisation. The children were still young and such a joy to be with and the social life was so friendly and nice. In 1982 Diane noticed a mole on my knee that had appeared and was growing. I thought nothing of it but I promised her I would see the Doctor who in turn referred me to a skin specialist in Stoke on Trent. One month later I turned up for my appointment and experienced the normal delays. At the time I was heavily involved with my sales team on a big deal and thought I would not bother with the specialist but then my name was called. Within two minutes he had arranged for the mole to be removed for a biopsy and told me the results would be no more than one week in coming. The nurse then offered a telephone for me to call home, something that hospitals would never do normally and to compound matters I couldn't get an outside line, further increasing my anxiety. My awful suspicions were aroused, because they were giving me special treatment. A week later the specialist broke the news to me. The mole was a melanoma – skin cancer. He explained that this case was very rare and unbelievably a second patient had been diagnosed in the same week. The diagnosis was a 50/50 chance of survival.

On reflection I put the illness down to 1964 when I travelled to Spain with my mates and spent 2 solid weeks on the beach. I was as brown as a berry. Did this cause the problem 18 years later and was it triggered by the stressful time at work? I will never know. Fingers crossed it has not returned and if it does any offending mole will be removed instantly.

Strangely I never once dwelt on the seriousness of the diagnosis. I spent 6 weeks in hospital recovering from the operation to remove a large area of skin from my knee, but did not have to undergo any chemotherapy because the removal of further skin was clear of any cancer. I always felt I would be up and about again and returning to normal life However it somehow affected my confidence and thoughts on my family and roots. Soon afterwards my employers offered me a less stressful job in their Head Office in Brighton so we moved down to Sussex, where we had left from 10 years earlier. This act of benevolence and goodwill was the last time I was to experience the generosity and support of a company I worked for, especially a Director at the time, Dick McLeod.

Windsurfing Bug

It was pre shanks days and my golf was still in good shape. But by 1999 the shanks came upon me and I turned to my other fascination which was windsurfing. Over the years I had tried to emulate those guys that speed out from the beach, complete a quick turn and return perhaps putting in a 'loop the loop' for good luck. My expectations were never to be that good but if I could at least go half as fast and return to the beach unscathed then I was up for it. I bought a basic board, sail and mast at The Worthing yacht club windsurfing sale and started on what is now a 10 year windsurfing experience.

Like all hobbies and sports that I have taken up before there is an initial period of tremendous enthusiasm, commitment and focus. Windsurfing was no exception so wherever we went visiting I had to have my stuff with me. Heaven only knows how the family put up with my paranoid obsessions.
Even today the first thing I do is look out of the window to judge the wind speed.
Interspersed with windsurfing I would take every opportunity to sail especially now I had less family commitments and the house was in very good order.
My new job introduced me to a number of very keen sailors and I remember well paying to join a yacht in the Solent competing in one of the Warsash spring racing events. I had absolutely no idea of what to do so they posted me next to the mast to help with the Bowman. I didn't gain much knowledge but it was nice to see the absolute astonishment on the face of a fellow work colleague on another competing yacht, which was the best in the race. It was a look of 'how the hell did you manage to get on that boat with no experience and no street cred'

So at every opportunity I would sail with my work mates chartering a boat in the Solent or over to France. As a crew member my skills were still extremely basic. I made all the usual mistakes. Leaving the gas stove on after making tea. Dropping the boom halyard before the main sail is up etc, etc.We all have to start somewhere don't we?

The Fastnet Race

In 2001 one of the guys at work said he wanted to compete in the Fastnet and was anyone else interested? He didn't have to ask twice. I paid the £1600 and received my instructions to qualify for the trip on a boat named Sigmaverick. The qualification entailed 3 race competitions to various French ports culminating in the Fastnet race in August.

The three races were good preparation and I was beginning to understand the rudiments of how a yacht performs and all its various functions but each trip entailed something different so it was difficult to assimilate knowledge and remember every thing.

But I do remember vividly the training trips as it was my first opportunity to complete a night watch on my own. I thought I handled the Traffic Separation Scheme very well and at one stage very nearly called for help. I saw a boat approaching us from the left. It had the usual two white lights for a ship longer than 150 metres and its green starboard light but further back there was a further white light. I thought this is a very long boat or there was another boat following it which gave us enough room to cross between them.

Luckily I erred on the side of safety and headed off to the left to avoid both lights. It then became very clear indeed. It was a towed boat with a 100 metre wire across. I know the French practice the guillotine but not on the back of a boat!

All three training trips went well and the crew of ten persons was portioned off into two watches each with a watch skipper. On the 8th August 2001 we gathered in the Solent ready for the off. There were approximately 200 boats and the forecast was for strong winds. As we sailed down past Yarmouth the wind had indeed increased to gale force strength. It was chaos with 200 boats trying to get through Hurst Point. One boat was dismasted and others in collisions. It was quite scary to see a boat rushing towards you doing at least 8 knots and tacking within 3 feet. By the time we had left the Solent I had spent too much time downstairs and began feeling seasick. I was told to lie on my back and let it pass over. In the meantime frantic sail repair operations were in place. The skipper wasn't holding back.

I remember getting back on the deck the next morning having managed not to actually cough up any sick, it was sunny and a F4 northerthly wind. What a difference a day makes.

The rest of the trip was quite uneventful. It took us 5 days and we finished in the middle of our class. Not bad for a crew of beginners. I'm glad I competed despite the seasickness incident, the Soya meals and endless packets of pot noodles. One of the crew was Marketing Manager for the makers of Pot noodles so the boat was stuffed full of them. You can guess I have never had another one since. The whole trip was a great adventure and gave me the incentive to attend evening classes for my day skipper theory.

Back to School

Colin Green our tutor was one of the old school. He had his own small yacht and would never agree to install a Genoa furler. He must have taught thousands of students in his time. A smashing instructor who didn't suffer fools gladly but would always offer that little bit extra advice and help to get through the exams. I had to re-sit my navigation exam because I took too many waypoints instead of adding up the vectors to make one combined vector - a simple mistake.

Now after attaining Yacht Master Ocean passage theory I look back with amusement, because I have always disciplined myself to use my theory knowledge whenever I go sailing. It's the only way to ensure it all sticks. I am far from perfect especially on tidal heights but at least I know I can passage plan as well as the next guy.

It was some 5 years after competing in the 2001 Fastnet race that I began to look further into sailing than just windsurfing. My job as Account Manager was very heavily commissioned based and I was working very successfully with my territory.

I managed to earn enough to buy an apartment in Fuertaventura after we had researched and visited many other places in mainland Spain and Turkey. One overriding factor was wind and windsurfing facilities. Spain was too expensive anyway and Turkey was too cold in the winter so we opted for Fuertaventura. It was and still is a lovely retreat from the stresses and strains of day to day living. I have spent many happy days and weeks there.

In 2005 my career suddenly took a nose dive. I was made redundant despite being the most successful salesman in the UK. The fickleness of Sales directors has always bemused me. A lot of his enemies must have used his decision to sack me as a weapon because he was later sacked himself. The embarrassment of getting the sack and the possible impact on one's confidence was not a worry for me. It was the most successful 5 years of my working career earning nearly a million pounds. Ask me now where it all went and I will hold my hands in the air, although 50% went into the government coffers.

It was a year too early for my planned retirement so I went for a few interviews with the competition. But I guess 59 years of age was just too much to overcome and the interviews didn't go well, especially when the MD of Compuware asked if I had done presentations many times before. What an insult. I should have taken down my flipchart and walked out there and then. Perhaps that was what she wanted for me to show guts and determination. Nonsense that's what I think. She had a strange motivation.

So I plumped for another option. It was a franchise named Technology Leasing. What a farce! They were based in Scotland and had built a very successful business in leasing to mainly local businesses. What they didn't know was how competitive it was down South. Their leasing rates were just ordinary and their Marketing prowess immature.

Nevertheless I managed to build my own portfolio of customers and leasing contacts with a good selection of competitive rates.

After 18 months I decided enough was enough. I put the business up for sale and came out without earning anything for 18 months. I now had my mind firmly set on my long term plan to buy my own boat.

The first step to heaven had begun.

First Step to Heaven - Let's choose a Boat

It's now 2006. I had retired and my finances were in good shape with a budget of £50,000 to buy a boat. I had already set my sailing plan out. I had dispelled the earlier idea of competing in one or all of the legs of a round the world trip, mainly because the cost was in the region of £26,000 for the world trip, whether it is with Chay Blyths lot or Robin Knox Johnson.

So I decided to buy a boat and sail around the world. First and foremost I needed to get some idea of what sort of boat to buy I started looking at all the obvious places

Yacht magazines

Boat brokers

Yacht yards

Web sites

Very soon I was beginning to understand the basics of boat design and their specific points. For example a bilge keel is great for rivers and drying out areas, but no good for blue water passage making. There was a marked significance in cost between different models and makes which took me some time to understand. Were the more expensive models depending on their reputation and name? Or were they genuinely different?

Even now I could not truly answer that question because I have never owned an expensive boat such as a Bowman, Swan, Oyster Discovery etc, etc. The most important research was in order to buy a boat that was seaworthy and comfortable in bad weather. I soon discovered two major classes of boat within my budget. One class was the older 'hand built' boats such as Nicholsons, Westerlys, and Moodys and so on. Alternatively there were the more modern 'mass produced' boats including Bavarias, Beneateaus, Jeaneaus and Dufours.

Amongst the hand built boats the Westerly seemed to offer good value but to get a 38 footer which was my preferred size, £50,000 wouldn't buy me a lot and maintenance costs I was sure would be a big factor.

In the production class I could get a lot more for my bucks especially the Bavaria's which appeared to offer excellent value. But how would a 38 foot Bavaria handle open water sailing?

I found the staff of most boat brokers very helpful. Although they had lots of production model boats on their books they still offered me advice and guidance on the different boats and their specific points of design. In general they confirmed that open passage sailing around the world would need a good sturdy boat but added that many buyers now purchase bigger boats for passage making so why didn't I buy a 45-50 foot Beneateau and still have change in my pocket.

After nine months of boat shows, boat yards and much deliberation I decided that a more solid hand built model was the best option so I narrowed my search down toWesterly's, Nicholson's and Moody's. I should add that I still had a romantic attachment to the Sigma 38 which was the boat I first learnt and completed the Fastnet race. They were a very good cruiser/racer but all the Sigma's I viewed were well used and in need of lots of TLC or they had belonged to one owner in good condition and above my budget.

It was at this stage that I realised £50,000 was just not enough to cover all the expense of buying the boat and fitting it out for open water sailing. Diane was also of the opinion that the most important aspect was safety since she would only worry about me whilst I was miles out on some Ocean. There were two Westerly Ocean Rangers on offer each for £66,000, which were way over my budget, but both very appealing. Unfortunately I couldn't get to see inside the one in Southampton and looking through the hatch I thought it looked a touch shabby. The one in Levington yard near Ipswich was available to view and I was impressed with its condition. Similar to buying a car I knew that wear on the upholstery was a good indication of use and the engine hours were only 600. So my mind was made up. I put in my offer of 60,000 which was immediately declined but managed to get the dinghy and outboard motor included in the original selling price of £66,000.

I had bought my very first boat at the age of 61. The boat's name was Dances with Waves. (DwW)I liked the name and decided not to change it.

Whilst the boat was out of the water I placed instructions for the local Rigger to replace all running rigging and standing rigging which was a pre-condition for getting the boat insured. Anyway the boat was 17 years old and needed new rigging. Also entry to the ARC would have insisted on this requirement. Also the rigger had said that quite a few local boats had completed the ARC with a twin headsail setup for the downwind sailing and the ARC statistics included many boats with twin headsails.

I asked the Rigger to set up this arrangement which was primarily an extra telescopic spinnaker pole placed on the mast. Finally I ordered the twin headsail and furler and a storm jib setup which involved fitting a staylock shroud that would be stored amidships alongside the mast shrouds. An estimated cost altogether of £9000.00.

I set a date of the 1st July 2007 to pick up the boat and sail back to Brighton Marina.

My best friend Mike who had never sailed before came with me together with Bob Hammond who introduced me to Sussex Yacht Club and the delights of racing around the buoys. Bob is a qualified instructor and very capable.

We arrived on the 1st July but the Rigger had not received my email to say when we were picking up the boat. The sails were ready the mast was down but no new rigging. To be fair the Rigger pulled out the stops and although we spent an extra night on the boat it was ready to leave 24 hours later.

I had already teed up Bob to say that I was to be skipper and passage maker and he should only offer advice if he sensed trouble.

On the 3rd July we were on our way with a plan to stop off at Ramsgate. It is hard to describe the mixed emotions of elation, expectation, joy, concern, perhaps a little fear.

The wind was a F4 westerly which was fine and I managed to navigate around Goodwin Sands without incident but the wind did change to a south westerly. But we still managed to reach Ramsgate. Here I didn't look up the depths inside the harbour and afterwards Bob did say that I went off to the right a bit too much which might have been a grounding issue if it was low tide. However it was OK I learnt a vital lesson. Just because you are within the safety of the harbour walls do not assume depths are consistent and marked.

Next day was sunny and windless but we did manage to sail through the straits of Dover. The reputation for lots of shipping was very apparent but again no incidents. From there we sailed a bit further and then decided we would need to motor if we wanted to arrive in Brighton Marina in a respectable time, which we managed to achieve.

My first step to heaven was complete.

Getting to know the boat

My first priority was to get as much use out of the boat as possible, especially as I was paying £750 per month in Brighton Marina for top summer rates. I didn't want to sign up for a whole year as I was hoping to get a cheaper mooring nearer Shoreham by Sea. My biggest challenge was getting the right crew together.

Most of my friends were casual sailors who only had weekends to spare and family commitments. What I really wanted were crew that could break away from work and offer experience with open passage sailing. It wasn't going to be easy because all the experienced crew already had their favourite boats and skippers.

After I had completed a few local trips out of Brighton with friends that wanted to see the boat, I began to despair about getting the crew I needed. Also Diane wasn't really buying into the sailing bit because she got seasick and couldn't enjoy the plus side of sailing i.e. freedom from the land, no unwanted phone calls, wind in the sails and all the glamorous bits of sailing. So I was beginning to think I will never be able to get my ARC crew together and time was pressing on.

In the meantime I continued to play around locally in Brighton and following a mooring incident in the marina decided to have a half day lesson in parking. This decision was the result of returning one day from a day trip and the wind was fresh. I steered the boat down towards the pontoon and as

I turned the wind caught the bow and turned the boat around. As I tried to get the bow back we gradually swept down past my pontoon and had to do a lot of reversing and manoeuvring. The owner of a large motor yacht shouted out angrily that practice parking was not allowed in the confines of the pontoons. If only he knew! Anyway after a lot of to-ing and fro-ing we managed to get parked with only a little damage to the pulpit of a very old wooden boat next door. I left a message to apologise but the owner never came back to me.

I completed my lesson the next week. Well worth the money. But nevertheless 3 years later I still have the odd problem when I don't concentrate on parking.

But back to the crew challenge, which never goes away, I decided if I couldn't get experienced crew I would recruit new guys and we could train together. So I posted a few notices around Shoreham Yacht Club and Brighton and I also advertised in Crew Seekers The local ads worked very well and soon I had a good if not experienced pool of people.

The message was very much 'let's learn together'. It was the perfect if not the ideal answer.

We started off just sailing and getting used to the rudiments then I entered the Sussex Yacht Club racing around the buoys weekend events.

What a revelation. I had very little experience of racing apart from The Fastnet and my crew had none. The first trip we lost the twin headsail and furler overboard because I didn't tie it to the guardrail. Bloody idiot I thought. There goes my first year's no claim bonus.

Anyway the racing was great fun. We had no pre-expectations. Just that we could compete and finish without too many embarrassing moments. Of course we could never compete on equal terms. Despite our handicap all the other boats were fitted out especially for racing, whilst DwW bless her was specifically designed and built for blue water sailing. Her keel was too small and she did not point up to wind at all well. Nevertheless all the other competitors were very sympathetic especially the Race Starter.

Each race was officiated by the race officer on the beach. He would raise the various racing flags and at the end note the times to work out handicaps and finishing results. Of course we always ended up way back from the boat in front. Each time I saw the last boat before us go over the line I would radio start control and say they could finish the race and return to the clubhouse. I was so impressed because every time the volunteer starter would hang on for us to finish. It was such a joy to hear the voice of The Race Officer as we crossed the line.

So 3 months after bringing the boat to Brighton it was time to get the boat on the 'hard' for maintenance, repairs and fitting of new equipment. My crew pool was growing and one or two more of the experienced crew were showing interest in my longer term plans to enter the ARC. Things were looking up.

Fitting out

With regards to fitting out the boat I had two priorities. Understand how the boat works in terms of repairing items that were faulty. They included a blocked stopcock in the aft heads. An ineffective pump for the forward Jabasco toilet and a worn toilet outlet pipe also. The engine had two loose baulk attachment bolts and the prop outlet had a small leak or ingress. I was beginning to pick up all these strange marine words such as ingress, gland, impeller etc, etc.

My technical skills were somewhat basic to say the least so you can imagine my trepidation in starting to undo and inspect bits of the boat that I didn't have a clue about, nevertheless I got stuck in. Perhaps this section is a bit boring but if you are as useless as me at technical prowess some of my experiences might just save you some frustration.

Turning to the forward toilet and pipe, one has to remember that of course the most important rule is how a thing goes together so that when you reassemble it all fits back nicely, which was my first mistake. Could I get the new parts working in the Jabasco toilet? Not a chance. Whilst I was on the phone to the supplier ITT Jabasco, I thought it rather odd, as I used to work for ITT in the long and distant past marketing hi-tech computers and comms equipment. How did they come to buy Jabasco? In the end they gave up trying to explain how their toilet parts work and sent me a complete new set. I was most grateful and impressed. So now I will always buy ITT stuff if at all possible.

Next the outlet pipe for the toilet, Simple enough job. Just replace the corrugated plastic pipe. Well sounds simple but the fit was so tight and working in a confined area doesn't help. Could I get the new pipe to slip over the stopcock? No chance. I must have spent two hours bending and persuading. I used a hair blower in desperation. In the end I met the local shipwright who sensed I was stressed out. I explained the problem. He casually said "you need to heat up both inside and outside the pipe. He was so right. Two minute's work and hey presto.

Onto the aft heads outlet stopcock. Apparently they are very prone to seizing up but no probs a good hammer should do the job if I could get some sort of decent access. Another day's frustration until someone else in the yard told me to get a long piece of wood, feed it up the outside of the hull outlet and tap the stopcock back into the boat. You've guessed it worked a treat.

Next the engine. I had taken a diesel engine course so felt fairly confident. Also my father always maintained his own cars including engine overhauls so I had learnt some rudimentary facts on how an engine should work. Also when I was 17 years old I bought a BMW bubble car and didn't check the oil on a trip to Brighton with 4 mates Yes 5 of us in a bubble car. The result was a blown cylinder ring which I replaced myself.

So I was very much up for servicing the 28 bhp Volvo 2003 engine. Also winterising it.

I ordered the parts from a recognised Volvo dealer which was my first real experience of the extraordinary expensive costs for boat parts. Now I know what owners mean when they say it's similar to turning on a shower with £20 notes flowing out.

The servicing went fairly well apart from the fuel filter which needs careful attention to replacing the gaskets. Make sure you put the new ones in the right order because they might be different sizes. Two further points of note. Buy a decent filter remover tool. I spent a long time trying to remove the oil filter until I went down to Halfords and purchased a tool that acts as a tourniquet around the filter. All you do is screw it tight and bingo it turns the filter case.

Lastly when you clear out the old coolant mixture for the engine the old mixture might not want to be drained off so might need to just turn the engine over for a few seconds to get the old mixture to pour out.

The more complicated bits such as replacing the worn prop gland and realigning the prop shaft with the engine I left to a qualified Volvo engineer who was based in the yard. I wasn't taking any chances with parts that come through the hull and need expert attention.

The second priority was to understand how the new equipment would be fitted and indeed work. This included a new GPS plotter and radar.

My electronic skills are nil so I thought it best not to install the wiring components of the GPS and radar but I did say to Barrie the engineer that I would fit the Radar box onto the mast and thread the wire down into the boat. Easier said than done.

For a start I am never happy with heights even though the drum was to be placed just above the first spar. So up I went and tried to drill holes for the bracket fitting. Eventually I succeeded. Now for the popgun rivets. This was proving too much because I had very little leverage to set the rivets. Back down the mast and back to the drawing board.

Barrie came to the rescue with a pair of ladders up the mast which gave a much better leverage and working platform. Why didn't I think of that? But we still had a problem feeding the thick radar wire down the mast. The in mast mainsail furler section left very little space for wiring so it was getting stuck 6 feet above the deck.

I had to leave the scene of the crime to go on holiday with Diane. But I later heard that with a lot of frigging around Barrie had managed to use an existing halyard to feed the mouse link of the radar wire down the mast to where it appeared just below the original blockage. Another valuable lesson learnt about improvisation. It would surface many more times.

Before going on holiday I had spent 6 weeks with the boat on the 'hard' from Sept to Oct 2007. Although it was dirty and there were lots of frustrating times I enjoyed the moment. There is something about sitting on the boat looking out over the River Adur and not having to worry about anything about work. It was an enjoyable time and to top it of I received a call from Sibella of The Riverside Yard moorings in Southwick. She owned two pontoons inside the Shoreham harbour complex and a spare mooring had come available for DwW.

She said "Mr. Thomas I have many owners waiting for a mooring but I do like your boats name so if you want the space let me know by tomorrow" I didn't even ask the cost I said yes instantly. My instincts told me the cost would be cheaper than Brighton and it was two miles from my home. What good news. Hopefully I could stay there without too much bother as Sibella has a reputation based on "three whinges and you're out". I would play the part of the wide mouthed frog when he met the Lion King of the jungle. Zip your lips little frog!

Back in the water

We finally launched the boat off the hard and motored down the river to Shoreham Lock. It was February 2008 and I was looking forward to a whole season of sailing with the objective of joining the ARC 2008. It was a bit ambitious because at this time I had many more bits to add to the boat. I had attended the London boat show and the Southampton boat show. It was whilst I was in Southampton I attended the Blue Water round the world seminar. It was strange to be the only single man at the seminar. The rest were men and their wives. Is there a message here?
It was well worth the money with very knowledgeable speakers covering all the different components of a boat from the type of boat, rigging, safety and power management systems. A couple who had just completed the trip were the main speakers and their experience totally changed my thinking. At this point I was dead set on turning left at St Lucia and going through the

Panama Canal as I really did want to see the Galapagos. So did my son Matthew. However the amount of preparation and finances involved with a circumnavigation made me think twice about taking on such a challenge. The couple highlighted the cost involved - £20,000 to get the boat ready then the same again to live and pay for running repairs. Ok they did say that savings could have been made if they ate on board more but my overall impression was having to invest at least £40,000 on top of my original purchase price of £66,000. This makes a total of £56,000 over my first budget limit of £50,000. I was beginning to comprehend the saying that it's a rich man's hobby, unless of course one has time and skills to complete all the prep work without the help of appropriate suppliers. But to me that is where gaps in safety and quality start to manifest themselves. This was proven to be very true over the coming two years. It was quite a disappointing moment. But not entirely ruled out.

Things for Passage making

The visits to London and Southampton boat show were most valuable. All the ad lines boast of how one can get instant answers to all questions from a myriad of knowledgeable people. I had a list as long as my arm and was determined to understand exactly what I needed for blue water cruising. It was fast sinking into my thick skull that open passage making is a vastly different kettle of fish to coastal passages.
By the end of January I had a list of major items I needed;

An adequate power generation system

A long range comms system

Additional safety equipment

Refrigeration

Water supply

Power consideration

I had already worked out the Amps that each power component might need. The biggest two items were the autopilot and the fridge There are many conflicting views about electronic autopilots (nearly all of which come from the ray marine stock). Mine was an Auto helm 4000+. The manual describes how the unit handles heavy weather without any mention of not using it in heavy seas. Yet some "advisors" were reticent about using the model in open passage making. I came to the following conclusion:

There were different electronic models to suit both coastal and open passage steerage. I believed my manual.
The alternative options were all very expensive such as the Hydravane at £5000.If I had the time I could have bought a second hand Monitor or something similar.
So I opted for my mainstay Autohelm 4000+. The decision is covered further into my trip.
Refrigeration was a fairly simple decision. The existing Isotherm was a top lid access fridge or rather cooler. It required an average of 3-4 amps to keep

stuff cool and an alternative front loading fridge would need acres more power, enough power to require a completely different power generation system. Perhaps loads of solar panels, and/or separate generator, and/or engine running daily. I was not expecting to have lots of cool daily beers on open passages. And the expectation was for fresh food to only last 4-5 days. Was a fridge really a necessity or a luxury? I decided against a fridge.

So my rough calculations for total ampage came out at:

Autopilot 4 amps

Fridge/Cooler   4 amps

GPS & instruments 1 amp

Nav lights 2 amps

A total of 11 amps per hour which could be reduced by 2 if I could buy a LED tri colour bulb.

I didn't include water pump amps which are a big factor if the showers are used regularly. Again I decided we didn't need to shower every day. However a water maker installation was still a possibility.

So how was I to get the extra amps I needed? The ARC stats were very mixed. Most boats had some sort of windvane. Some had generators and solar panels. Some had towed generators which were popular in the ARC because windvanes are not very effective downwind. A lot of boats had a mixture. DwW had a small Transom therefore Solar panels would need a decent A frame set up. I wasn't keen on using a generator mainly because on a small boat the noise might be a problem.

The Duogen is a dual system of power generation. It has a towed propeller that can be changed into a windvane when in port. Its statistics were impressive even when I reduced the manufacturer's stats to allow for 'not all perfect condition'.

Comms equipment

My VHF had been playing up since I first picked up the boat. The installed VHF was quite old and looked ready for the knacker's yard. So top of my list of priorities was to buy a new VHF transmitter/receiver.
This would not be sufficient for long passages as the best distance on a good day is reckoned to be no more than 25 miles. I was lucky to get 2 miles with my existing receiver.
I had a number of options for longer distances:

Satellite phone (with or without PC connectivity)
SSB Radio (with or without PC connectivity)
SSB radio with a Pactor modem

I spent a lot of time gathering information from various sources. What would we do without the internet and database engines? What a revelation, so much information.
My budget constraints were a major factor. The satellite phone offered the simplest solution because it didn't need technical expertise to install, test

and use. However the transmission costs were very costly just to make a standard call. Then the cost equation increased exponentially with the installation of a data connection. The standard bandwidth is 9.5 bauds which I knew from experience was very slow. Ok there are suppliers offering encryption and compression facilities but out there in blue yonder you can expect lengthy delays downloading weather information. Further information on this choice is covered later.

Now for SSB radio. Yes it is widely used and proven technology but VERY expensive to install unless one has the engineering/electronics know how. Also the government (MCA) insists on a Radio Licence which together with the training and licence cost of £80 will set you back some £500. And that doesn't include possible accommodation costs for the 4 day course. Again I will cover this in detail later together with costs associated with email and fax facilities.

Safety equipment

All boat owners should ensure that their boat is completely bullet-proof in terms of safety. Similar to insurance cover just how much safety does one need?

The various boat shows advertise thousands of safety systems and equipment. I don't think there is an industry list of items to cover mandatory to optional so the decision is very much down to the skipper/owner. I remember well the first skippers meeting I attended at SYC (Sussex Yacht

Club). The spokesman was covering requirements for the main events of the season and asked for a show of hands as to who had VHF radios.

I was astonished to see that at least a third of the audience did not raise their hands and uttered words such as "never needed all this fancy technology". Presumably some of these skippers owned small yachts that only competed in local round the buoys competitions but nevertheless what an extraordinary statement about boats at sea, safety and why the RNLI play such an important service.

My safety standards choices were made for me. The World Cruising Club (WCC) organisation running the ARC were very specific about what the boat should have ranging from dual speakers for the VHF through to System B life raft as a minimum. The very first thing I bought for the boat was 4 lifejackets and a spare VHF aerial and that was before I picked up the boat in Levington marina. I later found out that I was far from covered for the first WCC inspection.

Refrigeration

Many owners put this requirement high on their list of priorities. Perhaps nowadays the boat is seen very much as the second home, so continuous fresh food is a mandatory requirement. The only item that I like is cold beer when we arrive at our destination. So as long as I remember to buy them before we leave and put some in the bottom of the cooler that's sufficient. The step up to full refrigerator status is a major power drain and quite a job to change the accommodation either for the fitting of a front opening refrigerator or an additional unit. On reflection it would have been a nice feature out in the Caribbean.

Perhaps I am being a bit basic in this area and today most modern boats come with standard refrigeration so apologies if I am out of step with progress here.

Water supply

Just like the previous subject what determines luxury or necessity? Of course fresh food should be stored safely and as long as possible healthily. Of course one needs plenty of fresh water at sea. Apart from tasting nice it stops dehydration, a common cause of seasickness.

Today our water supply companies spend millions of pounds ensuring we have healthy drinking water yet we all buy bottled water to drink. What's wrong with tap water in this country? 30 years ago bottled water was unknown and we could also drink water from fresh water streams. I suppose the days of polio and, legionnaires disease have left their mark.

My premise was that the tanks were perfectly ok for drinking water, but if anyone on board was not happy with that arrangement then by all means buy bottled water.

Despite my opinions the plan for the ARC was to use bottled water for drinking and the tank water for cooking. Washing up water would be from the sea and personal hygiene would be simply baby wet towels.

At this stage I had not entirely discounted a water maker but the general impression was:

- What if the water maker fails on the first day of a 30 day trip?
- Do we really need to have showers and personal washing?
- The boat has enough room to store enough drinking water for 4 men over 30 days.
- A water maker has an improving reliability record but is still prone to breaking down.
- The better and more reliable models were coming out at £4000.00 plus excluding
   Installation costs.

The cost equation finally put me off, although at one stage I was tempted to buy the Mactra manual water maker from Macro which was about £2000.00 and proven technology. If it can service rowers traversing the Atlantic in an open canoe surely it must be up to the job.

The 2008 season begins.

I now had a boat that was fitted out and ready to go back in the water. It was February 22nd and I had accomplished as much as I could to at least get some serious sailing in and continue with my preparations for the ARC Rally.

I also had the beginning of a good pool of people for crewing. It was a mixture of crew that wanted to increase their sailing skills and had passed their day skipper and yacht master and the original beginner's crew. I felt a certain fondness towards one or two especially Matt and Gill. Gill is from Glasgow, very determined, charismatic and full of fun. Her partner Matt, a keen Chelsea supporter is the perfect foil for Gill, bringing her back down to earth every time her ideas got too much out the box. David is a complete beginner and prone to sea sickness but 10 out of two for perseverance. He would not let it stop him from coming out.

The experienced crew added they right mix and since they were not seasoned open passage sailors still had plenty to learn just like myself.

The plan for 2008 was ambitious. A sail every weekend with longer trips mixed in between the local round the cans. I attended the SYC skippers meeting at the same time as getting the boat back in the water and signed up for the starter roster. That was going to be a challenge understanding the different flags and signals. SYC also held a training session in March which was very useful.

The first of the local races started in March so we were soon on our way. As mentioned earlier DwW is a solid cruising boat and despite the handicap system didn't have a cat in hells chance of catching any of the competitors. But we all enjoyed getting out there and all the crew were learning useful skills. During one race we were rafted up in the Lock with all the other competitors. Next to us was Bojangles a very serious racing yacht that had one accolades during Cowes week. I was chatting to Jill who was my

Commodore when I first joined SYC. She remarked on the size of our GPS plotter. I thought of the Bishop/Actress repost joke but thought better of it. I now realise why she made the comment. In racing you don't carry any excess weight and a big GPS was deemed so. Serious stuff.

What's more important we didn't crash into anybody.

The Royal Escape

Our first serious race to Fecamp

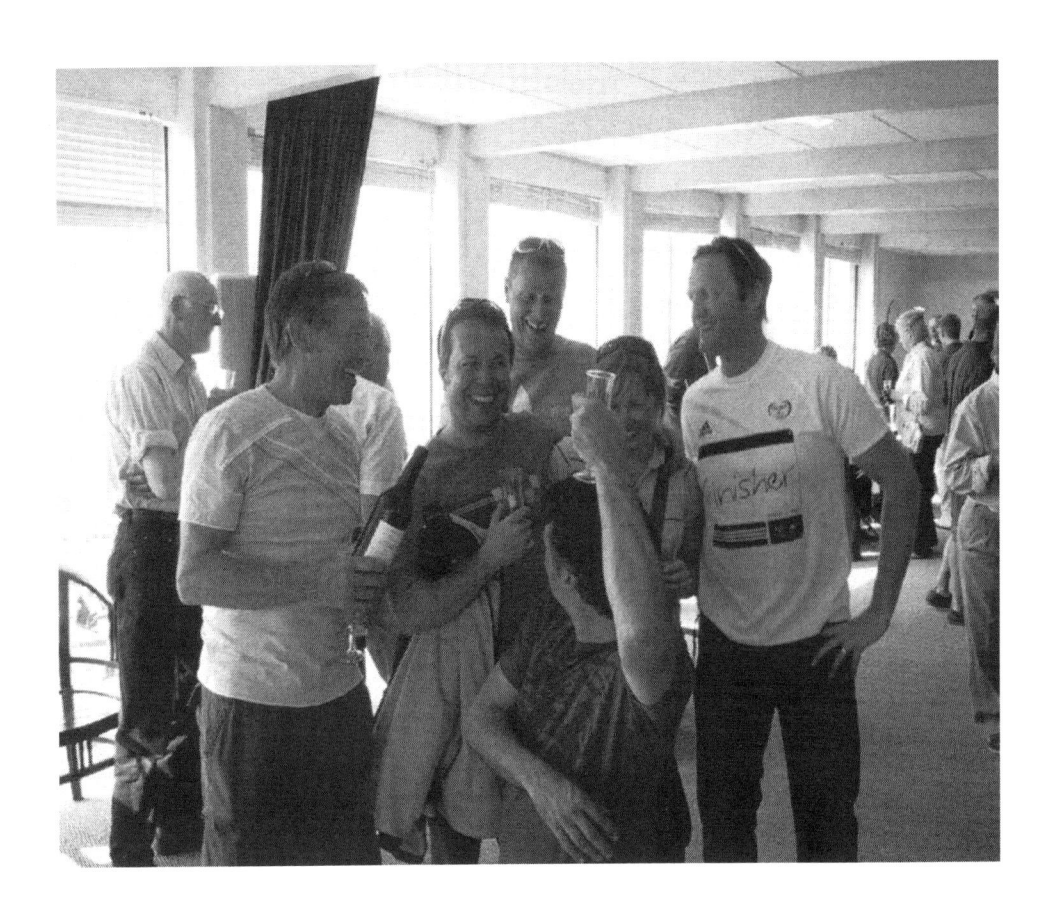

Although the local races were a good grounding for sailing the boat under time restraints and pressure, the first big test for me as skipper was fast approaching. It was the first big event for all the local yacht clubs including Eastbourne Brighton and Littlehampton. The Royal Escape celebrated the abdication and flight of King Charles 2nd to Fecamp and 70 plus yachts left Shoreham on the 1st May.

The week before I was very busy ensuring I had all the necessary safety requirements which included a further 6 man life raft to support 6 crew, instead of my 4 man liferaft. Also I did all the provisioning or victualling which is the traditional word.

It was quite a sight to be setting off with 70 boats of all sizes. There wasn't much wind which was not good for our heavy displacement boat so we were soon left behind. But we didn't revert to the engine and the wind did eventually increase. The 72 miles took us 23 hours. Which included a short period of engine power at the very last stages because the high hills around Fecamp blocked out what little wind there was and we would have been parked outside for sometime waiting for some favourable wind. As it turned out we were not last and arrived with no major incidents. It was a good to get my first skipper passage successfully under my belt.

The Channel Islands' trip

We continued competing each weekend and then set off for Portsmouth to join the RYA sponsored trip to The Channel islands.

We were 4 crew including Marcus who had passed his yachtmaster coastal skipper and two ladies. Pam had previously sailed around the world with the Robin Knox Johnson set up. She had decided that the duties of Mother, foster mother and grandchildren were no longer her priority and wanted to do something that would wrench her out of her overwhelming family commitments, which a circumnavigation of the world would certainly do. Pam is the ideal crew member, always positive, great communication skills, unselfish, always ready for the call to arms and a good sailor. She hates engines and would always sail everywhere including into the marina.

Marcus had already intimated that he was interested in the ARC so in a way had seruptitiously filled the 'first mate' position. Marcus is a builder by trade bought up in a working class environment with very strict social ideals. Very similar to myself but whereas I had continued studying and worked in a commercial environment Marcus was very much your self made tradesman. He learnt in the University of Life and understood the less positive sides of the human race, whereas I always thought the best of people. Although we had very different interests in life we made a very good partnership which held up well over the coming months.

June the 1st we met up with the other RYA rally boats and Peter a young lad joined us from Sutton. He contacted me through crew seekers and was keen on increasing his day skipper skills. So off we set on the 1st June under engine as there was absolutely no wind. We almost motored all the way to Cherbourg which was a shame. The next day we were told the Rally was staying in Cherbourg because strong F6/F7 winds were forecast. That didn't suit us staying in Cherbourg for one day is enough let alone two. So we agreed with the rally skipper to meet up with the fleet in Guernsey in two days. We planned to leave sharp at 8am to firstly catch the local Cherbourg peninsula tide and then the infamous Alderney Race with our destination Jersey.

The passage plan worked out very well and we zoomed through the Race showing 11 knots on the boat speed. Eventually the tide turned and we had a long session rounding Jersey on the west side. The east side looked too intimidating with all the rocks showing on the chart. Nowadays I wouldn't blink an eyelid but this was only my second passage. We arrived in Jersey at 9pm to find St Helens closed except for a local Indian restaurant. A long but successful day.

The very next morning we set off from Jersey to catch the west going tide to Guernsey and arrived in St Peters Port at 2pm where we rafted up with another Westerly. The rest of the fleet began arriving later in the day after experiencing a lovely F4/F5 wind. The forecast of F6/F7 never transpired but there you go better safe than sorry.

Of course we were now a day ahead of everyone else so whilst they spent the next day in the marina we decided to sail across to Sark. It meant calculating the tidal heights stats very closely and by the time we set off I was very concerned how much clearance we had. My heart was in my mouth as we approached the sill but a local French sailor shouted out that the sill was half a metre deeper than advertised. I still don't fully understand his words but we cleared out without incident. Phew. That was not the end of our day's adventures though if only I knew what was coming up.

The sail to Sark was only a couple of hours and we anchored in a nice little bay some 200 yards off the beach. Marcus was keen to get ashore and climb up some 300 feet above the beach. I looked through the binoculars at the beach and was concerned that the shore break looked quite lively. But not daunted we launched the dinghy and outboard and left Marilyn and Pam on board. I jumped into the dinghy with Marcus and Peter dived in alongside us. As we approached the beach we saw the shore break but were not put off. We should have turned tail there and then. The first wave took Marcus off the front of the dinghy and as I tried to steady the dinghy the second wave completely capsized the dinghy. A few seconds later I surfaced holding the broken handle of the outboard motor.

We all managed to get on the beach together with the swamped dinghy. Much to my regret I didn't take Marilyn's advice to put the VHF and mobile in a grab bag. Both were inoperative. The outboard was also water logged and wouldn't start.

Not too be put off we decided we could row back and set off up the hillside. On the top we met other hikers exploring the island sensibly by foot. I'm not sure what they thought of three people bedraggled and soaked to the skin. Soon it was time to get back to the boat and to launch the dinghy off the beach. I wasn't looking forward to the event. As it turned out we did ok with Marcus rowing and Peter and I swimming and pushing the dinghy. Thankfully the tide was not a problem. Pam and Marilyn were in fits of laughter when they saw us approaching the boat with Marcus on his knees paddling with one oar and his lifejacket fully inflated which gave an impression of a warrior Viking attacking the boat. I couldn't understand why my lifejacket hadn't inflated when we capsized. I later sent it back to the manufacturer. They fully tested it and passed it "Saying that some of the later lifejackets do not inflate until they have been submerged for duration of seconds". My ducking felt a lot longer than a few seconds. We then set sail back for Guernsey forgetting in all the excitement that we had earlier approached the Bay by way of a transit. Suddenly I noticed an unusual active wave ahead. It was the rocks that the transit avoided. I have never turned that wheel so quickly before and managed to miss the rocks.

Later that evening we had a reception in the Guernsey yacht club and one of the locals confirmed that hundreds of visiting boats experience overturned dinghies in the Grand Cuvee bay? I wish he had told me that morning.

But that was not the end of this fateful day. On returning from the reception I asked Peter to help me fill up the water tanks. I went to turn on the tap and when I looked for Peter he had disappeared. Suddenly I heard a shout from another boat saying "someone has just gone down into my boat". The next thing I saw was Peter being thrown off the boat we had rafted up to. There was complete pandemonium as the wives of the adjoining boats starting screaming and shouting. The police arrived and found that Peter had not stolen anything but had entered someone else's boat without permission. The policeman asked me what I was going to do. With the boat owner shouting expletives at me and the women saying they didn't feel safe with us in the marina I had some decisions to make.

Peter's story was one of "I was caught short and thought the other boat was ours". I didn't believe him as he had been on our boat for four days and would certainly have recognised another boats interior.

Pam believed him and said we should let him stay. I was more concerned for the safety of the boat and having a possible unpredictable person on board. So I decided to let him stay overnight and then get the ferry back in the morning. We untied the lines and moored outside the marina on the visitor's pontoon. There were no electrics on the pontoon which brought about another adventure later on in a few days.

Peter slept in the cockpit and left the next morning. He left me his mobile phone as a replacement for my drowned one. This was a kind thought but I had made up my mind and the safety of the boat came first.

We set off with the fleet and sailed to Alderney. Again it was a windless day and motoring through the Alderney Swinge was not a problem. 5 hours later we moored to a buoy in Braye harbour.

Alderney is a special place for Pam. She has inkling to live there one day with her friend. We didn't see Pam again until the evening at the final rally reception. We had been told the story of how her friend likes her tipple and always calls for refills with the words "fetch the mushroom soup dearest". I must confess the island did seem an island of lost souls or sailors. It was Friday lunchtime when we explored the town and already people where falling over.

But that doesn't detract from the friendliness of the islanders and the lovely countryside.

At the reception everyone received a prize. Ours was an inflatable pink dinghy. Very apt I thought. Overall it was a well run event with an experienced organisor ensuring everyone was safe and happy. I was surprised to meet fellow skippers who had spent many years sailing the Solent but never ventured beyond. This event was a major happening for them and some repeated the rally every year.

We left the next morning heading for Shoreham some 100 miles away. It wasn't long before we hit the unofficial TSS with a number of big boats crossing our path.

For some reason which I can't recall presently I tried to switch the engine on.

There was complete silence with just the solenoid clicking. The batteries were flat as pancakes. I rushed down stairs to see the batteries reading 11.50V.

Then I backtracked our movements and it occurred to me that we had not had pontoon power since we left St Peters port marina. Since then we had moored up in Braye and Marilyn had been reading in the night.

I assembled the back up battery nav lights and hoped that by the time we reached Shoreham we would have some sort of power.

Of course I now know we didn't stand a chance because the motor has to charge the batteries and we had no way of starting it.

It was an anxious 12 hours or so for me and as we approached Shoreham we made plans to sail into the harbour. There was no thought of calling the coastguard. I did call Shoreham harbour control as we were within 5 miles but they called back to say the Pilot boat crew had just gone off duty. Thanks pal. So I said we were coming in under sail which is strictly not allowed in Shoreham port. He didn't say a thing.

As you can imagine my thoughts and mind was in a stir to say the least. The thought of entering a narrow harbour with no engine was a new experience. Luckily the forecast for strong swesterlies had not yet materialised so we gauged our tack and heading and set a small Genoa reef only. At this time there was a calm F3 swesterly.

The first bit through the entrance was completed without incident now it was down to getting in the lock. We approached very very slowly and fortunately we were using the large commercial lock because the small boat lock was out of action. We sailed in and managed to secure a rope to the dockside of the lock.

I told the harbour man that we were not able to sail the boat into our mooring, it was much too narrow and winding, and so he agreed we could tie up on the other side of the lock until the morning although normally this practice was also strictly forbidden.

So this we managed to do by hand towing the boat through the lock and around the corner alongside the two pilot boats and the boss's new safety rig. By this time it was early morning we'd had very little sleep and were soon awoken by the new duty harbour man telling us we had to move as he didn't want to be told off by his boss for mooring alongside his new rib. I was in no mood for these unhelpful tactics after such an ordeal but I did call Barrie the engineer who was on the boat by 8.30 on a Sunday morning with a spare battery charger. Within seconds the battery was up and running and we moved the boat onto our mooring.

Moral of the story is please VOLVO start putting a hand crank feature back on your engines. I later discovered the Alternator wasn't charging the batteries anyway because the previous owner had wired the alternator up to the 12v cigar lighter. No wonder we had no power.

The remainder of June, July and September were taken up with mostly local "racing" and a couple of French trips to St Valery and another Fecamp sail. The St Valery rally was undersubscribed with only three boats, DwW, Barda and Moonlight Saunter which is owned by the very effervescent club captain. They were so pleased we came along because it takes at least three to make a race. In fact the captain Birdseye as I fondly call him awarded DwW a third place trophy at the end of the season. He was mindful not to mention that third place was also last place. I was just so pleased we gained some recognition for our efforts.

The Dutch Trip

It was now 31st August and we set off for our sail to Holland. The crew was the same as the Channel Islands with an additional fifth person named Bill. A 70+ years something character. He was a great addition with always a smile and a story to tell. I became very fond of Bill over the coming months. We set off in a brisk F6 swesterly which continued to be the main weather pattern throughout the trip. Soon we were up the English Channel with Dungeness on our port side. It seemed to take an age to get near Dungeness and we decided to cut over to the French side. By evening we were approaching Calais and making way up the coast. It was a Friday night and must have been the beginning of the last weekend of the summer holidays because I have never encountered so many ferries coming and going from a port. Every twenty minutes one would enter and the same for leaving. The approach channel was like Piccadilly Circus with two ferries crossing each other next to us in the approach channel. It certainly forced one to adapt to and accept having large boats very close by.

We arrived in Calais 18 hours after leaving Shoreham, too late to get into the marina but we weren't that eager to explore the town. I certainly had visited Calais on many occasions by car during the booze cruise era.

Next morning we set off up the French coast. Winds again swesterly F6/F7. So we made excellent progress. Apart from the rain which had now set in but only intermittently. We planned to stay in Nieuwport, Belgium. Motoring up the approach to Nieuwport we noticed a number of Statues of favourite pets on the channel marker poles, first a dog then a cat. I'm sure there is a story to this amusing spectacle.

It was still early evening but very wet and the town centre was way back down the channel entrance, a good 2 mile walk. Pam, Mo and Bill decided they were wet enough so just Marcus and I walked into town. No matter how nice a town or place might be the rain and dismal weather seem to lower the enjoyment. On another sunny day I'm sure the centre would have been more appealing but this day, No.

The third days sail took us into Dutch waters. Compared to French and Belgium waters the Dutch are very strict on immigration and visitors. We were met by a Dutch Customs boat that radioed us and instructed us to moor alongside the customs dock before doing entering Breskens Marina or anywhere else. Their instructions were officious but friendly.

By the time we arrived they had already moored on their dock so I went on their Launch to present our papers, during which time the girls were enthusiastically chatting up the customs crew. What is it about women and men in uniforms? After a very stringent check of our papers and reasons for being in Holland I returned to DwW to find the girls were already in the middle of a conducted tour of the customs launch. I think the girls were offered a shower and night on the launch with the Dutch men. But the crew had more duties to perform so off we went and moored up in Breskens.

I remember the visit well. We ate in the clubhouse and it was the best Sea Bass I had ever tasted and the other boats in the marina were in another class. Beautiful big new yachts, Classical wooden gaffer yachts faithfully restored and shiny with lacquered veneered wood all over. There were a few million pounds moored up in that marina.

The next day we set off for Vlissingen more commonly known as Flushing which was about 7 miles north of Breskens across the Westerschelde. It's here that the first canal begins. We could have continued up the Dutch coast to the Friesian Isles but we wanted to spend our time exploring the enormous stretches of the inland waters. I had purchased all the necessary maps which came in a 1 inch to a mile scale so close up enough to highlight all the usual navigational marks. We didn't experience any problems getting to Flushing apart from avoiding all the massive containerships going across our path. Presumably on their way out to the rest of the world or on their way in to Dutch and German ports. The experience made the English channel TSS seem like a stroll in the park.

We managed to navigate into Flushing and find the Walcheren Canal entrance in amongst all the docks and harbour activities. We spent 40 minutes waiting for the bridge to open and let the south going traffic come through. It was our first sight of a Dutch barge that had been converted into a living barge. It must have been at least 80 feet long and 20 feet wide. Just enough room to traverse the width of the bridge opening. But I guess this mode of transport had been around longer than man can remember and everything fitted perfectly. We found out later that delays at the canal entrance are just part of a cunning schedule to tie in with the other locks further up the canal. There is a very good guide on sale to work out all the lock times which would be a very good buy if one was staying any length of time and studied physics to understand it.

We motored up the Canal with plans to stop in Middleburg. I had not adjusted to the sense of mileage in these canals and before we realised we had passed Middleburg and popped out at the end of our first canal. Luckily there was another very pretty town at the end with temporary moorings. So we went alongside and walked into Veere town.

It was an old castle town with some of its walls still standing which had been restored to a very high level. This was a lovely introduction to our first inland marina and Dutch town, especially as the sun was shining on this day.

Pam and Marilyn were not convinced that I passed Middleburg by mistake. They were more convinced that I didn't want to spend time shopping in the much bigger town of Middleburg.

So we sailed on to reach the first big waterway. Stopping off at a small marina named Kortgene, another very friendly town and a very welcoming bar where Marcus, Bill and I spent a few pleasant hours tasting the local brew.

It was the 5th September 6 days since leaving Shoreham. We left Kortgene to sail to Goes but first we wanted to sail up to the vast expanse of the Oosterchelde Sea to view the Oosterscheldekering Bridge which spans this enormous stretch of water. Once again the weather wasn't at its best so we didn't get the best views. By the time we had completed our sail and reached the Lock to the Goes canal it was tipping it down. Once again we had to wait on the visitor's pontoon for the Lock to open. Bill was on the pontoon when the green light came on. I quickly started the engine and didn't realise Bill was behind me with one leg on the boat and one leg on the pontoon. It was a close call but not as close as the next incident. Because we were late leaving the waiting pontoon as we approached the Lock the lights turned red. We were so close to the lock gates that I decided to put my foot down and GO. The back of the boat was 6 inches from the gates as they closed. I looked up into the control tower and realised there was no lock keeper. The gates must be controlled at another lock further along. How else could they not have seen us so close to getting squashed? Oh well all in a days sail. As they say.

Goes was some 5 miles up the canal and despite the torrential rain was a very picturesque trip. Well worth the effort because when we arrived in Goes we came across this beautiful little marina. It had lovely grass gardens and picnic tables. The club house was almost like someone's house with large easy settees. And pretty ornaments and pictures. We couldn't fault any of the facilities not just here but all the places we had stayed in so far. Goes is a large market town for this area and the night we visited there were hundreds of young people riding into town for their night out. They were all friendly, happy and helpful. Everyone had their own bikes including all the young girls. What a difference to our Friday night booze night in the UK. Yet also here youngsters could quite legally visit one of the cafes or shops to buy their 'smokes'. I was most impressed with the Dutch culture. It put our culture and values to the test.

The next day we departed to sail to the eastern end of The Oosterchede and entered the canal to return to Westerschelde. We carried on down to the Vlissengen waterway and followed the Channel back to the North Sea entrance. The channel was marked with the usual red and green buoys but at times they were a mile wide. We were followed out by a large Tallship that went north of us keeping close to the Red buoys. We kept to the left hand side of the channel following the Green buoys. As we approached the Vlissengen area I noticed two large commercial ships pass each side of us.

Twenty minutes later we were hailed over by our friendly police launch insisting we follow them into Vlissengen Harbour. They looked in a serious mood. "Do you know why we have instructed you to accompany us" said the officer. I had no idea except that we had not paid our marina fee in Kortgene. That's not the reason he said. By this time I was becoming rather concerned. He then explained that we had travelled up the wrong side of the channel and they had received a complaint from a vessel saying we were a danger to shipping. This was a very serious offence that had a fine of at least 2000 euros. Now I was worried.

I kept to my usual tactics in this sort of predicament; doff one's hat in shame. Show innocence, plead ignorance and ask for forgiveness. In the end they relented and sent us packing like badly behaved schoolchildren. We left Vlissengen as quickly as we could but just couldn't get out into the North Sea due to the strong tide and F7 wind on the nose. The police launch radioed us again but I replied that we were having difficulties leaving and were changing course to head back across to Breskens. That was the last we heard from them. Thank goodness.

We departed Bresken at 08.30 on the 8th Sept to sail all the way back to Shoreham. The familiar SW wind F7 was now on the nose so after 12 hours we decided to divert to Calais for the next night. But then the wind backed to SSE F4 allowing us to sail down the English Channel. So we sailed during the night making good progress. 30 hours later, at 14.30 hours on the 9th Sept the wind veered to the SW F6/7. But by this time we were far enough down the English Channel to have the SW wind on a broad reach and head over to the English side. We arrived 36 hours later in Shoreham.

A smashing adventure and one to be repeated eagerly in better summer weather hopefully. I think Holland is a wonderful area to visit and next time we will make it to Amsterdam either by allowing more time to go through the lakes and locks or by sailing via the Friesian Islands on the North Coast.

Now back in Shoreham and no further distance passages planned I was determined to make best use of the boat before the winter set in. So we joined the next SYC Rally to sail down to Littlehampton and stay overnight at the invitation of Littlehampton YC. This is traditionally the last major event of the year for SYC so is always well turned out.

The idea is to ask a nominated skipper to race the boat back from Littlehampton to Shoreham approximately 15 miles on the Sunday after the Saturday night Club dinner.

Joe was nominated skipper for our boat. We were rafted inside a number of other boats so had to wait our turn. It is always amusing to see the boats leave as there can be a very strong tide on the river. Without fail the first boat left and managed to bang into the boat ahead of it whilst trying to fight the tide. Joe managed very well partly because a number of boats had cleared the way somewhat. But not to take his glory away he could very easily have tripped up. The race back was hard work owing to a less common easterly wind on our nose. This made us a lot slower than the rest of the fleet who managed to catch the last lock before low tide in Shoreham.

Out with the anchor whilst we wait for the extra couple of hours for the next favourable lock. This doesn't always happen but if there is a spring tide and opposing atmospheric pressure then the guaranteed lock depth of 1.9 metres can be optimistic.

The remainder of September and beginning of October we completed local racing around the buoys. It was good practice for all the crew and increased their sail setting skills and my skills at judging when to make the turns. Sounds a basic skill but believe me very hard to judge when to tack for the optimum gain.

During the Autumn Series 6 it was very rough and confused seas and on our way to the first turn we heard on the VHF that two boats had collided with one boat suffering a dis-mast and beaching, yes actually beaching, and the other a large hole in the bow. What I find so positive is the way the owners take such incidents as the norm and unlike other sports do not complain and point fingers rather than just shake hands and get on with it.

It was now the end of October and perhaps just time to make another longer passage and I wanted to visit Bologne a favourite French town that my eldest brother Mike visited often. Mike had always enthused about buying a boat albeit a motor launch. He lived life to the full and always said he wouldn't live much past 50 due to his larger than life excesses. He did manage to live to the ripe old age of 59 whilst he was living on his old Princess motor Launch based in Gibraltar. He died in 2002. Five years before I bought my boat so he never lived to see me realise our dream to buy a boat together. I do miss him so and think about him a lot whilst sailing. He was very selfish really to indulge so much when he had a family that loved him to bits. But that was Mike. What you saw was what you got charisma and more charisma.

So off we set for Bologne on the 29th October 2008. It took 22 hours due to another easterly wind against us. Why oh why does the wind always blow against us? If we had decided to go west down to Portsmouth the wind would have changed to a swesterly.

The crew was a bit nonplussed with Bologne but it was a sort of pilgrimage for me personally. To visit the walled city and enjoy a pint of Stella just as I did with Mike was sad but so nice.

The next day we sailed to Dieppe. Again I have fond non sailing memories of this town.

On one trip I took my two boys then aged 13 and 14 for a proposed bike and camping holiday.

I had borrowed my next door neighbour's aging bike so when we ventured into the French hills above Dieppe.the boys left me standing and as they do disappeared into the distance.

4 hours later we managed to meet again and picked a spot for the night's camp. It was on a slope and I was volunteered the lower part. Before we could get the tent erected I asked Matthew where the poles were. They should have been in the bag he replies. But they are not I said. He shrugged and walked away. I got my old scouts skills together and crafted a couple of very shaky poles. By this time it was absolutely tipping it down and the tent

was leaking. Of course muggings here had the lowest position so all the water was ending up in my sleeping bag. By 2am we all decided this was not a good idea and hotfooted it back to a nice warm Ferry Terminal. We returned on the first available boat.

This little episode might seem to the reader that we had a disastrous time.

Yet in all honesty we all enjoyed the adventure and learnt lots of lessons. Riding in the French countryside rather than motoring was a lovely refreshing change.

So back to the boat and a last look at Dieppe before we set off back to Blighty. On the way back we actually had a southerly on the stern so we set the twin headsail and Genoa combination. It worked well for a time until the wind changed to ENE yet again but this time it helped us get down to Shoreham in 16 hours a total of 80 miles.

It was now early December. We completed a couple of local Christmas Cracker races. Marcus had not sailed since Holland so suggested we have a few days in the Solent. He arranged to meet us in Portsmouth as he lived in Marlow.

Pam and I set off in a favourable Northerly wind and with the tide with us easily made the Inner Owers Gap with 3 knots of tide behind us. Then the wind dropped and I put on the engine. About three miles from the Horsesand Tower the engine warning light came on I rushed downstairs to find the impeller unit gushing out water. It was pitch black outside and many commercial boats coming into the Solent.

However Pam sailed the boat well whilst I inspected the Impeller. It had completely torn to pieces and needed replacement. Within a few minutes and with much swearing I located a new impeller and replaced the old one. Panic over we continued into Portsmouth harbour. The next day we motored to Yarmouth with no wind and plenty of fog. My first experience of the stuff. Quite eerie but good to use the Radar in case of a ferry crossing our path. It only lasted a couple of hours so no big deal.

The next day we set off for Chichester Marina. What an adventure that was. At this time of year it gets dark by 5pm so we entered the Chichester waters in the dark. Marcus had previous experience of Itchenor so he was familiar with the Channel.

By the time we reached Itchenor it was getting very foggy and misty but we had to motor on to get the lock at Chichester marina. The harbour master had informed us that with a depth of 1.5 metres we would have clearance up to 6pm. The final leg between Itchenor and Chichester was unlit so it was a bit of a lottery especially on the bends. However we arrived at 5.45pm and seeing the lights of the lock entrance, turned right to commence following the green posts to the entrance.

Suddenly the boat ground to a halt. We had touched the bottom. Desperately I tried to reverse out but to no avail. Quickly we jumped up and down on the deck but still no good. The green posts marking the entrance channel were only 20 feet away so we pumped up the dinghy to row over and secure a couple of holding lines for when we started to topple over. By this time the ebb was well and truly on its way out and despite the dark we could see the bottom of the mud.

Unfortunately whilst we launched the dinghy off the back of the boat it caught the life raft stays and the life raft fell into the remaining water and started to drift off down to the river. During my panic moments I fell into the cockpit locker which is a good 6 feet deep. Thankfully a broom broke my fall and avoided a more serious broken leg.

It was too late to secure the ropes on the pole as the water was too low so I decided to try and paddle after the drifting life raft on the other side of the boat which had a bit more water. I rowed some 30 yards and gave up because the life raft was going faster than my paddling and the rope securing my return to the boat was getting waterlogged and sinking. It was a fruitless exercise.

We accepted our fate and waited for the boat to topple over. I rang the harbour master and gave him a few selected expletives. His response was that we were not close enough to the channel posts to maintain the very small dredged channel.

After another hour we could see the last remaining water drain off. The boat was on a 45 degree tilt but holding its own with no superficial damage. The channel was indeed very close to the poles and if we had stayed within 3 foot of them would have made it. Thanks harbourmaster for not offering us a tow off the sandbank and for not telling us to keep close to the poles.

Going through my mind was the local press turning up the next morning and taking pictures of us stranded. Most embarrassing. As it was the Tide was gaining height rather than waning so 6 hours later we had the clearance and good old DwW slipped off back into the main river with no more to do. We then went up the channel and moored on the Chichester marina visitor's pontoon. By this time the nighttime/nightmare harbour master had gone off duty and I thought it pointless having a go at the daytime staff. I wrote the incident in their logbook but never received an acknowledgement or some sort of sympathy type response let alone an apology. Oh well lesson learnt. Next time I will do my own tide calculation.

There was a happy ending. We didn't get our photo taken and the life raft ended up alongside the marina wall. Marcus returned with mud up to his knees and one intact life raft.

It will take a lot of persuading for me to return to Chichester Marina.

The next day we returned to Portsmouth and Marcus departed leaving Pam and me to sail back to Shoreham. I delayed the trip 24 hours due to an unfavourable forecast for gales in the Channel. It didn't materialise and was still forecast. We agreed to take a chance and set sail. The wind never exceeded F7 and was a swesterly which gave us a great sail in big swells all the way back via the Inner Owers.

Quite an adventure for just sailing to the Solent and back.

The year was a great success for me personally. I had now completed over 2000 miles as skipper and owner and despite all the mistakes we had finished with no major disasters and a very capable cruising boat. I emphasize cruising rather than racing because the SYC prize giving party was all about the rally and local racing successes, although we did get a third prize cup for the St Valery Rally. I shouldn't really blow my own trumpet especially as we were only three boats competing. Well at least it gave the other two a chance to officially compete in a race (the rules say you must have three boats to gain status as a race)

I think Captain Birdseye (alias Captain Skinner – the mainstay of the club) of Moonlight Saunter felt we deserved some recognition for at least trying. So we did get a couple of very nice engraved whiskey glasses one of which I gave to Dave after he was presented with them. A small token of my thanks for his support and endurance.

February 2009 - Fitting Out for the big adventure

The Solent trip was the final sail of 2008 and it was now time to start getting ready for the ARC 2009. By the end of 2008 I had a very clear idea of what I needed to do in readiness for departing Shoreham on the 21st May 2009. Here's a quick rundown of what I thought:

Crew

The ARC team was firmly fixed and consisted of Marcus who was first mate although we never used the title in practice. Marcus was committed to completing all the 6 steps of the journey to the Caribbean and back. His plan was to complete the passages and return to the UK to re fill his finances. Diarmid lived in Aberdeen and owned his own Dufour moored in Larges.

His objective was to experience an open water passage to give him the springboard to sail his own boat to Norway in 2010. As he had not met any of us he planned to travel south in the spring to meet us all. I met Diarmid through crew seekers and chatted a lot about his sailing experience, work and family. He appeared a very sound and reliable person. Chris the fireman was the fourth member. We had sailed a few times in DwW and like me on a very steep learning curve. Very capable person, reliable and great company always full of life and so positive. It took Chris a lot of manoeuvring to wangle the extra weeks from work but his boss signed off the time and he was determined to join us.

To get favourable terms I also signed up for two other World cruising club (WCC) events. They were the Portugal Rally and ARC Europe.

Rob Graham another sailing beginner was pencilled for the Portugal rally subject to getting the time off from work. So with Marcus and me we had the team fixed for Portugal.

Provisioning for the ARC

I spent some time trying to speak with other owners who had completed previous Arc's.

One local lady explained how as dedicated cook she planned for the 3 weeks at sea.

It was a useful couple of hours and enabled me to get a list of all the bits that make up the requirements. But more importantly what we needed to get before we left. Many countries including Europe do not sell cans of pre-cooked meals such as stewing steak, mince and baked beans etc,etc.Also very English things such as Branston pickle. I still had to work out just how much we needed for 4 grown men, but most importantly how much water to take. Some sources recommended 3 litres per person per day. Others said 2 litres. I had decided against the water maker and instead rely on sea water for washing up and baby wipes for personal hygiene including washing. This left the water tanks dedicated to cooking. In the end we settled for 2.5 litres per person over a period of 30 days. This equated to 300 litres of bottled water.

The other main item bread was never covered in my initial planning. As it turned out we found a place in Gran Canaria that could provide pre baked baguettes with no need to keep in a fridge. I now wonder how many preservatives were in the mix? It certainly did us no harm and the baguettes cooked beautifully in the oven after 10 minutes or so. Since the ARC trip I began making my own bread. It also worked very well and would have been a very good method for long passage making. It certainly made a change from the sweet soft bread sold in the Caribbean. I think we provisioned for 3 per day x 30 baguettes for the ARC trip. It worked out well because we had a few left as one would expect as the trip was only 20 days.

The other provisions of note were the tins of food for main courses. I calculated we needed 1.5 cans per day which is 45 cans consisting of mince beef, chilli, sausages in beans, meatballs, stew. This was more than enough because we had at least 15 cans left after the trip. I'm glad I made the effort to visit a local wholesaler compliments of the SYC who loaned me their membership card for the day. It enabled me to stock up with all the bulky cans and durable food such as peanuts, packets of rice, spaghetti and pasta. Some items we overstocked because of minimum carton amounts but the exercise was very worthwhile.

The important thing to remember is that the food intake is far less at sea than one would expect. Certainly for the first few days we only ate basic stuff such as bread, cereal, cheese, ham and fresh fruit. The first few days always are the same. Speaking personally it does take me 2 or 3 days to get my sea legs and my appetite is much reduced. I found during the trip that Marcus and Chris two 15 stoners plus didn't eat anymore than Diarmid and myself 10 stone plus guys.

Also the first 4 days at least should be covered by fresh food bought locally. We didn't have a fridge but we still managed to have fresh food for 4 days.

Of the fruit, apples kept very well whereas bananas were soft after a few days. Eggs last very well also. We remembered to keep turning them each day which must have done the trick because we only just ran out after 20 days and could have had another couple of dozen on board.

Our best buy was a huge Gouda cheese wheel. It was a very nice addition with ham, biscuits and nuts or crisps each evening. The wheel stayed fresh and lasted 19 days.

I could go into a lot more detail but really provisioning is a very individual choice and the best option is to try and gather as much experience from other people and then make a decision involving all the crew in the planning.

Power management

As detailed earlier I needed to supply at least 11 amps per hour to feed enough power for the fridge, autopilot, navigation and instruments. The duogen towed generator specified a minimum 8 amps at a boat speed of 5 knots increasing to 10 amps at 6 knots. The plan was to switch off the fridge at night so maximum amps would be 4 amps for the autopilot and 2 amps for navigation and instruments. I also purchased a 45 Watt Solar panel which should generate 1-2 amps during the day. So all in all we should not have to use the engine to generate enough power.

I fitted the Solar panel on the deck between the mast and the bow. Barden the supplier promised the panel to be durable enough for crew to stand and walk upon. The installation was very straight forward except for the wiring which had to be fed through the deck down to the saloon and through the panelling into the instrument and navigation where the batteries were placed. I then fitted the regulator onto the main instrument panel. I had decided not to install the optional excess power overflow regulator as Duogen hinted that sometimes it would take over the other regulators and dump electricity before the Duogen for instance was still charging. This was my first exercise in drilling holes into the bulkhead and connecting units. I was rather careful as I was not to know just what might happen.

Marcus came down to stay for a couple of days to help fit the Duogen unit to the stern. This went Ok apart from Marcus's over zealous approach to fitting the drive bolts which have a very fine thread. The second bolt was cross threaded. Engineered metal bolt fittings are not quite the same as screwing Phillips wood screws. Marcus is a builder by trade.

I sped across the yard to Barry the marine engineer who returned with his re-boring tool and cut a new hole for the bolt. It's easy when you know how.

So now we had power source independence. My only concern was the extra weight now fitted on the stern; which had the Duogen, life raft and outboard motor attached.

Comms equipment

My final decision was to install the SSB Radio and also purchase an iridium satellite phone.

SSB Radio

One of the most popular radios is Icom. It's also the most expensive. But Mactra offered a brand new Yahatsu for under a £1000 nearly half the cost of the Icom. Being aware of my quickly increasing budget costs I plumped for the Japanese model. Mactra did explain that it was a USA model and should not be used in the Mediterranean. This was not a problem because I would be outside of this area for my travelling.

I took time to study all the available information on how to install SSB. The Yahatsu documentation was OK but the technical requirements to fit the comms equipment were very daunting, especially installing copper wire for grounding and insulators for the whip antennae. I contacted Eurotec in Brighton who quoted £1300 to do the lot.

They fitted the hull attached copper block and wiring inside the boat. The tuner was also fitted near to the stern to ensure a proper conduit to the whip antennae on the backstay. The engineer dialed in some German station and gave a nod to say everything was in order. Who was I to say otherwise?

My license and 4 day training program were fixed for April 2009. The course and license cost totaled nearly £500. An old friend lived near Southampton and he was so good to put me up for the three nights. Accommodation cost with a package through UKSA would have added another £500.

So all in all the SSB option had cost me £200 short of £3000 excluding training accommodation.

By the time I had sorted all this lot out my enthusiasm for researching how to buy and install a Pactor modem was just about at zero. My initial look at this option and my basic knowledge of modem transmission put a number of doubts in my mind. I knew from experience that data transmission outside of commercial use hadn't improved or advanced in many years and the software packages although very cheap didn't look very exciting. But all said and done the financial argument was extremely good compared to the satphone solution. Nevertheless time was running out so I opted for the easier satellite phone option to obtain weather reports.

Iridium Sat phone

During the winter of 2009 I had also researched the Sat phone option and purchased a second hand Motorola 9500 phone for £600. This model was not the latest but I was promised by various suppliers that it would have data comms capability. Fortunately my work years before with ITT data transmission did give me some basic rudimentary knowledge of data communication technology. The phone came with an excellent package of manuals two good lithium batteries, battery charger, various international plug fittings and a Sim card with some credit units still remaining so I could at least test the basic phone. It all worked perfectly.
Now comes the hard bit. How to get the phone talking with the PC.

I still had to get the phone to work with my PC so I could download weather information and send/receive emails.
I had met Ed Wildgoose of Mailasail a couple of times at the boat shows and was impressed with their focus on providing just sat phone based solutions. They offered a very straight forward package to supply the software. They did not supply the data comms adaptor for my older sat

phone model but I wasn't about to buy the latest 9501 model at a cost of £900.

Some time later after many phone calls to find a supplier that had the 9500 data adaptor I wish I had purchased the 9501. Eventually I tracked down a supplier in the USA that had one. It cost £250. I never found out how much one would have cost for the later 9505 but I did find out later that a UK supplier had them in stock for a mere £40.

The email software was £140 pounds and the phone calls came in blocks of 50 minutes costing £75 as a minimum. I later purchased the 500 minute block for £750.

Now I had all the bits for completing my sat phone requirements. I tried to get everything working as an initial test but couldn't get any satisfactory test results. Mailasail were very good and supplied me with one remaining bit of kit. It's called a serial adaptor which converts the data from computer mode transmission RS 232 to phone transmission. My test results worked. So I put everything on hold until I needed to buy the £750 airtime. I did ask the other 3 crew if they were prepared to share this cost 4 ways to enable them to stay in touch via phone and email during the 3 weeks of the ARC. After consulting their partners or in Marcus's case children there was a very positive yes.

The cost to get this service up and running was:
Basic sat phone £600

Data adaptor £250

Software £140

Serial adaptor £40

Total cost: £1030.

The success of this comms option was unequivocal but I still had a few bridges to cross before it all worked. Because I didn't have enough of the existing SIM card and the small amount of test minutes supplied by Mailasail I left full testing until we left for the big adventure.

Eastbourne Trip

Keen to try out our new look boat I organized a weekend trip up the coast to Eastbourne. The SYC were also visiting that weekend for the regatta. So it was nice to see them. As usual the wind wouldn't play ball and even if we had enough to sail the SSE coming across our bow so we motored all of the 43 miles. I somehow expected Eastbourne entrance not to dry out but we arrived at low tide and needed to navigate up the narrow channel to reach the entrance lock. On the way I had noticed a rattling from the prop shaft but the engine sounded perfectly Ok. The next day still worried about the shaft and returning home I donned my summer wetsuit and tried to dive under the hull. Although it was early April it was so cold that 1 abandoned this idea. Ian the morris dancer and a qualified diver got chatting to a local dive boat that had just returned from a dive and were already kitted out. Ian persuaded them to have a look at the prop shaft. After a few moments they reported nothing wrong with the prop shaft as the anode appeared to be loose I came to the conclusion that the shaft Anode must have worked loose. I do recall that during the last fitting out Chris the fireman replaced the old anode and found it difficult to screw the new one tight. Was this the problem?

We set off for Shoreham and once again the wind wasn't playing ball as it was now a traditional swesterly on our nose. On with the engine and despite good revs the current around Beachy Head was doing its best to send us back to Eastbourne, and we finally passed Brighton Marina after 8 hours. The next day in Shoreham Marina Ian donned his diving gear and tried to fit a new Anode. It was bitterly cold and he couldn't manage to tighten the retaining screws as well as he would have on shore. Nevertheless a gallant attempt and one I was grateful for.

So a few days before, and on the way to Plymouth to meet up with the Portugal Rally I tried sending emails using my usual Microsoft Outlook. No way could I make it work. At our first rally briefing in Plymouth I met other Mailasail users with similar problems.

After a few frustrating phone calls with Mailasail we set off for Bayonne still without an email service. Of course we could still use the sat phone basic telephone service so we could call the rally organizers in the Isle of Wight with our daily position. The penny finally dropped during the Portugal rally when Mailasail pointed to a major installation instruction in the documentation. Use Microsoft Outlook Express which I had already installed as part of my Microsoft Office product. I set up a new Outlook Express account which was so simple and Bingo we were in business with full email services.

The final trip in the UK

It was now May 1st and just three weeks before the big off. We completed one more trip as part of the SYC Solent Rally. The start was delayed owing to very poor visibility. But I knew we had little chance of getting any medals so we went on ahead. The fog gradually lifted and we made headway to the Solent via the Inner Owers. By now I had a good measure of what to plan for getting through the Owers and on to Portsmouth. So despite a Swesterly wind we managed to get the sails up and gradually the wind increased to a F7 gusting 42 knots. It still needed the engine on to get through The Inner Owers. We arrived in Portsmouth 13 hours later.

The next day we enjoyed a nice sail with the Rally and sailed to Cowes. Our problem was injury and sickness. I was suffering badly from a chest infection, Nic had a very sore hip from the previous day's exploits and Ian was feeling under the weather. We all met in Cowes in The Little Island YC. It was a very poor reception indeed. The management had left all the hospitality to very inexperienced staff. The beer was flat, the food cold and the makeshift Marquee very drafty indeed. We decided to leave the Rally reception and head for the local pub where it was nice and warm.

The next day we were all suffering some sort of ailment so due to my chest infection and not wanting to jeopardize my big trip we decided not to stay with the Rally in Itchenor. So back to Shoreham a day earlier than planned.

It was an excellent sail. Averaging 7 knots.it took us 8 hours. As it turned out I'm glad we did return early. On the way home from the boat Ian suddenly fell ill and was rushed to hospital with a duodenal ulcer.

Second Step to Heaven - We leave Shoreham for Plymouth

Dances with Waves starts her adventure from Shoreham Lock

It's May 21st 2010 and time to leave on the second step of my adventure. The plan was to join up with the Portugal Rally in Mayflower marina on the 26th/27th May, which gave us time to attend rally briefings, provisioning and most important pass the safety checks.

The crew consisted of Marcus who decided to join us here instead of Plymouth, Chris the fireman and his partner Julie. Ian had to drop out following his illness after the Solent rally trip but was hoping to join us on our return trip from the Azores to England. That seemed a very long way off.

We left on the 0800 lock with a swesterly F5/6. As usual with the prevailing winds we had to tack up wind to go west and abandon our plan to reach Poole for the first night. Instead we rounded the Outer Owers at Selsey Bill and headed for Portsmouth. It was a very strange feeling to see the Shoreham power station tower disappear beyond the horizon for at least another year.

Next day we left Gun wharf Keys and tacked down the Solent in a SW F6 gusting F7. Some water under the gas stove set off the alarm. Not sure why? So I disconnected the alarm. (Fault no 1) This was the first of many breakdowns and incidents over the coming months. I was about to experience the taste of being a long passage maker and the ups and downs of maintaining a boat which is constantly on the move. We joined the Poole Approach which is a long way out from the harbour but spotted the channel marker and south cardinal easily enough. Moored up in Poole Town Quay amongst the big shots. The Sunseeker boys. The expensive mooring fees reflected the affluence which was very apparent but did not reflect the quality of facilities.

Saturday May 23rd depart for Weymouth and Portland.

Managed to sail most of the 5 hours. Took photos of the famous Osmington White Horse and Rider cut into the hill in 1808 under the auspices of John Ranier, brother of Admiral Nelson.to commemorate various Royal visits to the area. The rider represents King George lll. Wasn't this the infamous Mad King George? We had a quick glimpse of Portland but decided Weymouth might offer more things to do as it was a Saturday night. We rafted up in the harbor, which was very busy and just managed to reach the pontoon electricity post. But a rain shower wetted the so called waterproof/bullet proof connection on the length of cable (remember I severed the cable whilst servicing the boat in the SYC yard) and tripped the fuse. Now every boat was without electricity. So we shortened the cable to avoid the connection joint and solved the problem. So much for waterproof connectors. Weymouth was a lovely town and marina facilities OK.
Sunday May 24th departed for Brixham in favorable NE wind but it wasn't to last and soon we had the engine on which remained on for nearly all of the 45 miles. On the upside it was a beautiful sunny day, Lyme Regis bay was like a millpond and 30 or so dolphins came to play. What a fantastic sight. Everyone took photos which is a good job because I couldn't download my camera to the laptop.

Monday May 25th. Took a quick detour on our way to Salcombe to have lunch in Dartmouth Town. Tried tying up to a free vacant pontoon but was soon shown the way off because it was for boats under thirty feet. So we paid for a mooring a little up river and spent a couple of hours around the town. I was beginning to realize just how much nicer places are as we travel further west. First Brixham and Weymouth with their old fishing port ambience, now Dartmouth with its river to explore and places upstream to discover. We continued to Salcombe, tied to a bouy and were visited by a friendly seal. Looking out on the hills each side of us was a pleasure indeed. Lovely houses and cottages. We didn't have enough time to get the dinghy out but I'm sure the town would have reflected the same welcoming feeling.

Tuesday 26th May. Lovely bright day but very misleading as we rounded the headland out of Salcombe. Suddenly under full sail the boat lurched right over. I thought we were going to broach. The wind meter recorded 45 knots. We managed to reef in before the next gust but the wind was still gusting F8 all the way to Plymouth.
Drake's Island presents an interesting obstacle to enter Mayflower Marina. There is a short cut through the Bridge channel which is ok between 1 and 2 hours after low tide. But I erred on the side of safety and took the east route around.
Arrived in the marina and Step Two to heaven successfully completed.

Third Step to Heaven-Rally Portugal

I was convinced that the boat would pass the safety inspection by World Cruising Club since I had spent a great deal of time following their safety inspection requirements in the rally Handbook. Wrong -
No serious set backs but they did point out a number of must have items. Each lifejacket should include a whistle and light. I mistakenly assumed that when I purchased them they would have everything included. Not so. In fact some of the cheaper lifejackets do not include anything except the bare essentials.
WCC also pointed out a number of advisory things such as having a boat layout plan for such things as stopcocks, tools and spare parts.
The whole procedure certainly kept me on my toes and made me think more about how the boat works.
Chris the fireman left to return home to Kent and would next meet us in Gran Canaria. Marcus and I were joined by Rob Graham from Cardiff. He had taken all his theory exams but lacked practical experience. The fourth member was Roger who had previously worked for WCC on their World Cruising Rally but now wanted to be a competitor instead of an organizer.
Based in Guernsey Kieran was an ambitious lad, very presentable, good communicator and keen to learn. Rob a typical doubting Welshman and full of wit and cheekiness.
Marcus stayed in the local hotel with his new girlfriend. The day before when the other crew were on their way we went out for a day's sail to the

local beach. Marcus and Mary were completely besotted with each other. So much in love it was almost too much to believe. Mary is a computer software trainer and travelled abroad extensively under contract to Reuters. Marcus was about to enjoy travelling with her on some of her trips as well as passage making on the boat. His world had been transformed from living in a mobile home working on building sites to a jet set traveler and ocean going adventurer.

There was talk of marriage after only a few weeks of knowing each other. Everyone on the Rally could see this open love affair it was so positive and romantic.

There were only 15 boats sailing down to Portugal so over a period of 3 weeks we would get to know one another quite well. I was surprised to see what a mixed bunch of expertise was present.

Ranging from skippers with lots of technical skills and experience through to new owners relying on outside support for problem solving. I liked to think I was somewhere in the middle. Not because I was technically qualified- far from it- rather that I wanted to solve problems myself. Perhaps this was because in the past I could never afford to pay other people and had to try and fix things myself. That said I did have to call in an IT guy to fix my PC. Which he did and we managed to get the Mailasail link up and running but very slow and keeps dropping out. A few days before and on the way to Plymouth to meet up with the Portugal Rally I tried sending emails using my usual Microsoft Outlook. No way could I make it work. At our first rally briefing in Plymouth I met other Mailasail users with similar problems.

After a few frustrating phone calls with Mailasail we set off for Bayonne still without an email service. Of course we could still use the sat phone basic telephone service so we could call the rally organizers in the Isle of Wight with our daily position .The penny finally dropped during the Portugal rally when Mailasail pointed to a major installation instruction in the documentation. I set up a new Outlook Express account which was so simple and Bingo we were in business with full email services
.

Despite having no luck getting weather fax on the SSB radio I did complete my first SSB radio transmission with Fair Encounter. The skipper was a retired Electronics engineer and knew how to install and work everything on his boat including installing his own SSB setup. I was rather jealous of his expertise.

I attended the rally briefing which together with the film show during the rally dinner detailed a lot of information about the trip. Where we were going, what conditions we might expect, how to stay in touch with each other and the Rally Control in IOW. I was very impressed with the organization. Very professional and very detailed.

We left the Marina and joined the start of our first long passage. It was the 31st May 2009 and very light winds. Although we did sail over the start line in second place and managed to pass Eddystone lighthouse by 14.30 but by 1700 we reverted to the engine until 06.45 and I began to think with 550 miles to our next stop fuel would have to be managed very carefully. Not sure what my fuel strategy was at this time. I must have assumed that we would be able to sail all the way since I had not added any extra cans at this stage. Then the wind increased to F3/4.

The rally organizers were expecting a daily position report but it wasn't long before we lost contact on VHF as the other boats were generally one or two knots faster than us so were steaming ahead. The power for the Iridium Sat phone was the 12V cigar lighter which on reflection was a poor method due to its unreliability. We lost any power from this so couldn't use the PC to report in. But I still managed to call the Centre by direct sat phone call to report daily positions. Meanwhile we also had the latest WCC yellow brick plotting device which was fixed to our boat in Plymouth so even if we had no comms the centre could plot our progress.

The NE winds continued throughout the night so we goose winged the main and Genoa and everyone had a good nights sleep during their shifts. There were many Container ships through the night but nothing too close and no odd lights to distinguish. The third day out the wind backed to the East with a F3/4. So far the Bay of Biscay was being very kind to us.

The third day was fairly uneventful. Everyone was getting into their routine and the large swells became the norm. Although Rob was for ever looking over his shoulder every time a large wave came from across our aft. I was unperturbed because I knew DwW could handle much bigger seas than this.

I was more perturbed by Rob's anxiety. He looked quite frightened at times. I wonder what long term effect this will have on his sailing enthusiasm?

We managed to make VHF contact with Fair Encounter which is another Westerly, a Corsair a ketch with two masts, a forunner to DwW an Oceanranger. They were approximately 4/5 hours ahead of us. Doh.

It's Day 4 and still little wind to speak of. The engine had 16 hours clocked up and I was beginning to think we should head for the nearest port which was Coruna to refill the tank. Every hour I was checking the fuel levels and guessed we might just make it to Bayonne. I was becoming very good at measuring the tank capacity which was good practice but a bit stressful.

Cape Finistiere took ages to pass. I can imagine it would be a real handful in rough weather but it was continuing to be very mild with a F1 wind.

Later that day Kieran or Roger as we now called him decided he wanted to take photos up the top of the mast. I also wanted to change the tri colour bulb to a LED light.

So up he went with Rob and Marcus hauling him up. The opportunity for them to wind up Roger the cabin boy was too good to miss. So we had 30 minutes of Roger screaming out. He had taken on too much for his first trip up the mast and was beginning to regret having embarked on such an adventure especially with rolling seas. Of course Rob and Marcus(Able Seaman and Master Bates respectfully) as they were now named were loving every minute to wind up this little upstart from Guernsey. I was named Captain Pugwash.

Eventually he returned to the deck after failing to fix the tri colour as the bulb was incompatible. But he did manage to get some really good shots of the boat.

This theme was being developed by Rob who had a keen hand for writing pros. His story and video of the trip was a joy to watch and the accompanying commentary deserving of a BBC comedy documentary. Better than three men in a boat.

I later learned that Rob was hoping to sell pictures to various travel agents so his video and camera work was also exemplary.

We now had 55 miles to go and I had worked out that the last 3 inches on the tank equaled 19 miles. There was 11 inches left i.e. 69 miles. It would be close.

It was 12 midnight on the 4th June and the start of our fifth day at sea. There was 7 inches of fuel left. Or 49 miles and we had 12 miles to go. Phew!

We actually arrived in Bayonne at 02.45am on the 5th June after completing 520 miles at sea. We had motored 42 hours from a total of 210 hours at sea. The Bay of Biscay had certainly been very kind to us. All my fears of enormous waves and treacherous seas seemed the stuff of sea stories and not relevant to us normal seafarers. A bit of an anti climax I suppose.

Tony will get you

The first night was our chance to meet the other 14 yacht owners and crew. I sat next to a very charming lady whose partner was sat at the other end of the table. Rob remarked on his rather large stature and intense glare. I thought nothing of it until the next day when we were sailing. Rob said the boat closest to us was sending a Morse code message. He shouted excitedly and said he knew Morse code from his merchant navy days.

I quickly picked up a notepad and Rob began spelling out the letters:

WAITUNTILWEGETTOTHENEXTPORTTONY.

By the end of the message the crew was in fits of laughter except me. I had been well and truly HAD!!!

The next day was a rest day with a visit to Santiago de Campostela. It was cloudy and rainy just like England but we were in Spain in June so where's the warm climate I asked myself. Marcus joined me on the coach but should have stayed on the boat and recovered slowly from his previous night's celebrations. Touring around any town was not his thing especially with a giant sized hangover.

The town is world renowned as an historic pilgrimage location. People from hundreds of miles away start on their pilgrimage walk and end up at this famous cathedral. The atmosphere despite the damp weather was so positive and friendly with people shaking hands and congratulating each other on their journey. There was a major celebration in the church with thousands of spectators joining in with the Mass and singing at the top of their voices with such freedom and vigour. At the end a giant snuff box holding a ton of incense was swung across the entire length of the Cathedral. It was attached to at least 200 feet of rope and secured by a large block and tackle arrangement. It looked very insecure and wobbly and I wondered how it passed any EU safety regulations? I guess the Spanish and French are not so EU obedient as we British. Good luck to them. It's nice to see such historic spectacles unfettered and as they really were hundreds of years ago.

Sunday 7th June. Awoken by a rat a tat tat on the bow. I popped my head up and was greeted by some people dressed as a Doctor, a medic, two policemen and what looked like a harbour master. They were the real thing. What have they done now I said to our audience? Marcus and Bob where not impressed with my lack of support for them. They were right. I should demonstrate support and confidence in my crew! They wanted everyone up on deck to question us about the previous night's proceedings.

Marcus explained to them that they had met up with two of the Belgian crew who were moored opposite of us and quite a lot of drink proceeded. Later that night on returning to the boat Marcus and Rob came across one of the Belgians struggling to get back to the boat. They carried him back and put him to bed. They were not about to return to town to find the other Belgian. They had already done one good turn for the day/night.

The policeman then said a man had been found floating in the marina by one of the other yachts and he had drowned. I was beginning to think we were about to be hauled off to the local constabulary. However the officials seemed happy with Marcus's story and presumably had already decided that there was no foul play and that the Belgian had either fallen in and drowned through intoxication or had committed suicide which is what the Belgian captain had hinted at due to the man's problems at home. Welcome to Bayonne!

I decided to have a go at windsurfing in the Harbour which was quite large. It really didn't work. The wind was gusty and there were too many boats in the way. This was to be a familiar problem throughout my adventure. Bah.

Monday we decided to have a days sail up the coast to the beautiful Ria Arousa and the protected Isla Ons. But as we travelled up the coast the wind began to increase menacingly with large breaking waves so we decided to return before expected gale force wind conditions were upon us.

Tuesday should have been departure day for Povoa but the rally was delayed 24 hours due to the winds and rain. An AD HOC tour to La Guardia, Tui and Valeca was arranged.

We did manage to reach Portugal albeit by coach. I was most impressed with the visit to a 5000 year old Celtic Village restored to its original setting on the Santa Tecla Mountain headland and approach to the Rio Minho. The improvisation and skills of these Bronze Age people was amazing. They had originated from the west coast of England and Wales and settled there creating a very prosperous and effective civilization.

Wednesday 10th June

WCC wanted the rally to depart from Bayonne and they left by car to meet us later in Povoa. The weather was supposed to get better so the rally didn't leave. That is except for us. We were all suffering from marina fever so DwW departed at 11.15 with a Swesterly wind of F6. As we left Bayonne behind us the wind backed to the south and increased to F7 gusting to 40/45 knots. We could only manage 1.5 knots pointing straight into the wind. The crew were not happy so we turned tail and headed back to Bayonne. It took us 5 hours going and one hour to return. The Rally guys had rang up from Pavoa confirming they were basking in sunshine. I was not a happy bunny. We must have been only minutes maybe an hour from getting favorable winds to take us on to Povoa.

We all left the following day and I noted this time we reached our previous position in two hours rather than 5. I also had noticed that when we returned to Bayonne there was a worrying rattle coming from the prop shaft and when we had left it no longer rattled. I was almost certain it was the Prop shaft anode that Ian had fitted the previous February in Shoreham. The second anode to fall off.

I radioed the rally and told them I needed to inspect the hull in Povoa for a possible Anode replacement. They took the details of the boat the size of the prop dimensions and arranged for the boat to be hauled out on arrival in Povoa.

I was about to experience a fantastic example of organization. We arrived at the harbour entrance and WCC radioed instructions to go to the lifting out dock. Here we were met by the local harbour master and marine manager. Within 20 minutes the boat was hauled out, a brand new Anode fitted and the boat returned to the water. The Engineer explained that the prop anode should be fitted one hand width from the P bracket to ensure it would not shake loose. He was exactly right as I never again had any problems.

That night we were entertained by the marine manager in the yacht club. He did us all proud. The other rally members left quite early but we stayed on and gradually were joined by the local people singing and playing their instruments. I think it was the partisan events of earlier that led to us bonding and celebrating such wonderful cooperation. I gave the marine manager £30 and that was accepted under duress. My faith in my fellow human was at a very high level that night.

Friday 12th June. Departed for Figueira de Foz with a very sore head after the previous night's celebrations. Should have been first over the Start line but some had their engines on which may account for us not competing very well in the passages between each stop. So far both the other two Westerly's had achieved some recognition. There was a good following wind so we attempted to set up the twin headsail. After much frigging around it was set but I still didn't know if we were doing it correctly. It would have been good to have an experienced sail setting crew member. Arrived in Figueira de Foz well behind the fleet and just managed to squeeze in for the sardine supper. The rest of the crew preferred to eat in town rather than pay 20 euros.

The foot pedal was still in need of repair so the next day I set off to find an ironmongers or chandlers to get some long bolts. I eventually found one and couldn't believe how old the place was. A little old lady couldn't speak a word of English and the shop was just like the old ironmongers of yester year. The two Ronnie's show covering the "fork handles, four candles" sketch was the image one conjures up. Hundreds of shelves and little boxes of screws and bolts that looked at least 50 years old. But we managed to sort out a few long bolts.

This little exercise had taken 4 hours and back in the UK I would be thinking "I haven't got time for all this messing around. My time is too precious". However here I was on a 14 month adventure, but who cares how long I spend looking for spare parts? If only I knew what was to transpire over the coming months.

Figueira de Foz was a very big town with a mixture of tourists and locals. I met up with Marcus and Graham in one of the many cafes. They had met with some girls from the town's Casino who were contracted to sing and dance at the casino. They were very impressed with our story of sailing to romantic parts and expensive marinas. But I decided to play the whole thing down by saying we were more like Romany travelers with an old boat and lots of baggage. The lads were not impressed. I don't blame them they were only doing a bit of innocent flirting and fun making.

That evening they got their own back. We arrived late at the Casino and rushed down the stairs to the reception only to find the door locked and everyone inside. Or so I thought. What really happened was that I had turned left instead of right and was looking at the reception as a reflection in the glass. I turned to find the crew laughing. What an idiot I was.

The evening Cabaret was excellent and the girls gave us a special wave to acknowledge us. Then a most extraordinary thing happened. We all went to have a go in the casino. I bought my usual small of chips so I didn't lose too much and Marcus bought a few chips. He had one go and put his chips on Zero. The wheel span and the ball dropped in the green slot Zero. He took the winnings and cashed them. What an evening. We turned in at 4am rather wasted. I never learn.

Monday 16th June. Set off to Nazares, which was an unscheduled stop because of the delays in Bayonne. Approaching the start line Rob noticed water seeping up through the floorboards at a fast rate. Panic broke out as we thought we were sinking. I quickly checked the water foot pump and surprise, surprise the feed pipe from the water tank had slipped off whilst I was trying to repair the pedal the previous day.

Panic over as I reconnected the pipe. Had an excellent sail to Nazares reaching 10.8 knots then we approached the final headland and the wind increased dramatically gusting 45 knots The twin headsail was attached to the stem fitting for the storm jib and as we turned into the wind to take the sail down it twisted around itself. Marcus managed under a great deal of pressure to get the headsail down but he said afterwards he thought he was about to get seriously hurt from the twisting effect of the strop and sail. Luckily the sail didn't rip but the strop was completely trashed.

I spoke to the UK rigger the next day and after I had sent a picture he explained this was known as a halyard wrap. He explained that the headsail should never ever be attached to the stem fitting. It should be fixed to the eye bolt on the bow. The one he had set up specially. It goes to show how easy it is too forget how bits work on a boat. I had just completely forgotten this simple procedure and as a result caused a self inflicted problem that could have had much more serious consequences.

That night we had a free night so we opted for a little restaurant in a side street. The landlady explained that the restaurant was closed to the public but we could join the party if we accepted whatever food they offered up. As it turned out the food was fine nothing special but then the other guests started getting their instruments out and singing old traditional Portuguese songs. Then a young lady got up and sang the famous Fada songs. She was very good and usually performs in big towns and venues. Everyone was getting quite inebriated including one particular male singer who had an Operatic voice. It was superb until the landlady climbed up to the highest shelf to fetch the special Brandy bottle. He was beginning to wobble a bit.

We became very friendly with a young girl and her parents. Both she and her father took turns to sing. I suppose it was a Portuguese traditional singing Jam. I have always been very impressed with professionals performing and doing something I could never do. This evening was no exception and I bought the FADO singers CD as I normally do at live gigs. I

know I sound like an old git but programs such as celebrity chef just annoy me so much. Amateurs trying to be professionals do not wash with me.
An excellent evening. Isn't it always the case with unplanned events?

Tuesday 16th June. Departed for Peniche a small fishing port. Some of us took the option to visit the Berlenga Islands on the way. I'm glad we did. They were beautiful and well worth a stop. We only had time for a passing visit. A strange phenomenon happened on the way. We noticed hundreds and thousands of crabs floating on the surface. We never did get an explanation but I guess they were migrating with the currents to other feeding grounds. We arrived in Peniche and rafted up. Marcus set to and repaired the water foot pump pedal. It was so damned awkward to get access so it took a lot of maneuvering. A job well done. His carpentry skills won the day.

Wed 17th June. Although only a small fishing town Peniche must have had some strategic value in the past owing to its well fortified fort. The local tour took us around the fort and gave us a good insight to the sea going power of the Portuguese in the middle ages. Led by a famous Navigator named Eric he discovered and claimed on behalf of Portugal parts of West Africa, Azores, Madeira, Cape Verdi's, Brazil, India and Japan.

Thursday 18th June. Off to Oierus up the River Targa. Apparently this new marina is favoured rather than the better known Cascais marina. We had a F2 north easterly on our stern so up with the twin headsail. Completed in 9 minutes. It's getting better! Superb sail and what a difference in the climate.

As soon as we turned the headland into the River estuary we noticed a marked increase of at least 10 degrees in temperature. A sure sign that we were well on the way to the Mediterranean.

Oierus was quite a large town with lots to offer the visitor including historical sights and beautiful gardens featuring statues of famous artists, poets and historical persons. I got the impression this north side of the Targa leading up to Lisbon was very influential and in stark contrast to the previous Portuguese towns and villages.

Next day I visited Lisbon via the local train which takes one straight into the heart of Lisbon. The whole town is dominated by the castle St Jorge high up on the hillside. A tour of this remarkable building will testify to the fact that it has never been conquered or overthrown, due to its position and fortifications and despite attacks from The Moors, Spain and various other marauders.

Rob spent two whole days taking pictures of Lisbon to sell to various magazines and travel/tour operators. Some of his shots were very good even for me to recognize.

Saturday 20th June. Off to Sines (pronounced Sinesh). Portuguese language has a very unusual pronunciation. Sounds very similar to Russian with lots of slurring. Nothing like the written word which contains a lot of similar words to Spanish.

The trip to Sines was very light winds so eventually we put on the engine and motored. This delay meant we didn't get to Sines until 9 o'clock and the pontoon party was well under way. I wasn't in the party mood to be honest.

Don't know why perhaps a little homesick or perhaps living on a boat makes a person more independent and less agreeable to socializing. Yet everyone else appeared exactly the opposite with much socializing, joking and general positive bonding. It's no doubt that the Portugal Rally is a great vehicle for meeting good friends and experiencing sailing at its best.

I do remember seeing Kieran (Roger the cabin boy) on the pontoon. Since jumping ship in Bayonne to join one of the other boats who offered free food and engine motoring costs, he had joined his best university mate who was crewing as well.

Then his rather irate skipper came across and said he was chucking Roger off, because he had drunk all his booze and didn't do his chores. So I had the onerous duty to take him back on board as he was originally signed up to sail to Lagos. As soon as Marcus found out he threatened to set about Roger if he stepped on board. He called Roger a "Ponce"

I was not having any of this 1st mate truculence and said I had a duty to take him to Lagos

The problem did resolve itself. Another boat, a catamaran which was owned and crewed by a strictly vegetarian family was very happy to take Roger on board.

The word Ponce did stick firmly in mind for some unknown reason. Perhaps it was a word I hadn't heard for a very very long time. I later discovered in the Caribbean just why it had a certain ring.

The next day we were once again entertained by another well organized WCC tour around the Vasco de Gama castle. Sines is the home town of

Vasco de Gama who is a national hero on the same level as Nelson or Winston Churchill.

His exploits as a discoverer and philanthropist brought him unprecedented fame and riches owning all the property and land around Sines. Eventually the Mayor and local enemies became so jealous he was expelled and sent abroad. Later of course all was forgiven and a great statue stands in the town celebrating this person.

Our last day before sailing to Lagos and a beach BBQ was organized by the rally competitors. Some how it didn't quite materialise partly due to the weather. The only event not to have been a great success.

Monday 22nd June. Long last leg to Lagos. Rob left us here to travel back to the UK as his 3 weeks holiday was coming to a close. We were joined by Marcus's girlfriend Mary. Most of the trip was engine on and engine off until we approached Cape Vincent. It's a tradition here to salute Lord Nelson. Not sure why because the Battle of Trafalgar took place miles away near Cadiz. So history has it the British led by Admiral John Jervis met up with the Spanish enemy (outnumbered 2 to 1) and took them on before they could join up with the old enemy France. At the time Nelson was a junior Commodore in charge of a small frigate but his heroics that day earned him his first accolades from Admiral Jervis. Finally reached last headland before Lagos. Once again the weather had the last say and wind suddenly increased to gusts of 40 knots. At least it's consistent.

Lagos here we come and Second Step to Heaven completed successfully.

4 things of note:

Despite the excellent sea handling of DwW's she is slow so remember to allow longer for trips.

Must get poles down as soon as wind increase suspected

Write down where you leave things on the boat. So many bits go missing in such a small and confined area.

Missing family but think of positives. This is a lifelong ambition, a 14 month holiday and a massive adventure.

23rd June. Lagos marina has a lifting bridge arrangement but affords priority to boats so we were not delayed while I registered on the visitor's pontoon. Managed to negotiate an extra 10% discount for the months of September and October. Their rates are very expensive but they are only one marina of a handful along the Algarve so it's a bit of a seller's market. Nevertheless the number of boats in the marina was significantly down on previous years and competition is very strong. Apparently the squeeze had also impacted the marina restaurants and they had all reduced their prices to be more competitive with the town's restaurants. All the better say I.

Also Lagos Town is an excellent location for holidaying and provides all the usual amenities.

The marina has some of the best facilities on the Algarve. With a very good albeit expensive Chandlery and repair facilities. I ordered a new Stem fitting and Pilotage book for Spain and The Algarve.

In the afternoon WCC organised a visit by boat to the Grottos and a look at the local bays followed by a great Beach BBQ for all the rally participants. The drink flowed well and everyone was in a very positive mood knowing they had completed their journey and made good friends. I was most impressed with the entertainment, a single singer with guitar of the highest quality. He got everyone dancing and singing.

The next day we attended the final Rally meal in the Marina compliments of the Marina management. Various prizes and speeches followed together with lots of final hugs, kisses and tears. The prizes were impressive with a couple of nice rugs which Marcus took possession of. He later claimed one for him which seems to add up to his general characteristic of 'snooze you loose'. This was not the first time I had noticed this attitude of grab what I can. Earlier on Roger had been given a bag of Portugal Rally tee shirts for when we all arrived in Lagos. Quite openly Marcus had opened the bag and taken 3 shirts for himself. His response was not of guilt but one of "they can afford it". Returning back to the Rug present I reminded Marcus that if he wanted to share the cost of entering the boat in the Rally he was welcome to a rug. He reluctantly handed it back. Lots of business cards were exchanged as we departed from the reception but I felt we would not see much of each other in the future. Renegade was off to Corfu, Roanda, Gilly B and others off to the Med. Dave with his boat Lara off to Albufeira and Andiamo crew flew back to the UK. Ben More returning to the UK with his boat. So soon after arriving then to return fighting against the prevailing NEasterlies. He was keen to return and tour Scandinavia. Perhaps he did not like hot countries?

Ron and Hazel on Naivasha invited us to eat on board the next day.

After all the fond farewells it was nice to chill out on the beach which is only a few minutes walk from the Marina and the day was completed with an excellent five course meal on Navaisha. In the morning Mary departed for the UK and a return to work and a rather tearful Marcus confirmed they were getting married after the trip.

Exploring the Algarve and Southern Spain

So now there were two. Marcus and I set off for a few days sailing before he had to return to the UK and earn some money to finance the next stage. Our first port of call was Portamao. We anchored up just inside the harbour entrance and got the dinghy and outboard ready. The first of many launches. I remember Portamao well. Diane and I spent two weeks in the Dom Joa hotel just outside of Portamao town over 35 years ago. What a difference. The town had grown so big.

I liked Portamao but the next day we had a day's journey to get to Aloha near Faro.

We arrived in good time for the current that flows out from Faro and Aloha. It can reach 3 or 4 knots so timing is important. Most boats take the left side into Faro waters. We took the right hand turn and headed for Aloha. Getting there was a bit like Chichester Harbour with twists and turns up the channel. Aloha harbour has very limited mooring and we were soon told to leave our first mooring which was the only one available so we anchored up outside and took the dinghy over to the town quay. Aloha is a very busy fishing port and buzzing with locals. I took to the place very easily and enjoyed the hustle and bustle of the arguing locals.

Next day we left for Albufeira and on the way I attempted to get a bucketful of sea water whilst we were sailing and was very surprised by the power of the water against the bucket. Determined to hold on it very nearly pulled me over the side. So I let go before it did and got off with a sore burn on my arm. Albufeira Marina is a good distance from the Town and we only had one night to spare so we stayed in the Marina. It completely lacked any heart and was more like an old dying marina rather than a relatively new one. They were obviously suffering from any new developments and all the new apartments were empty. Their marina office was still a converted mobile home arrangement but in an attempt to get new arrivals their rates were very attractive. I was now persuaded to ditch the idea of spending the summer here and convinced Lagos had so much more to offer. I could understand Dave of Lara wanting to moor here because he would be returning to the UK regularly. When we left Marcus pointed to the building on the hillside which took the shape of a large passenger cruiser.

Next day we returned to Portamao and this time carried on further up the harbour and anchored off a small fishing village called Ferruggo. Nice friendly place but not very cheap for a small remote village.

On our return to Lagos we visited Alvor which is literally 2 miles down from Lagos. The veggie family had anchored in Alvor as it was well protected and free. It was not yet an official summer holiday period for Portugal so the channel was not marked as mentioned in the Pilot Book.

Notorious Alvor, Portugal

As we tip toed through the harbour channel entrance we had difficulty eye balling the town quay as it was very flat with no landmarks. We carried straight on which was very nearly our undoing. Suddenly the depth dropped to 2 metres. So we quickly reversed and returned to deeper water. Fortunately a small fishing boat came past and spotting our dilemma and pointed to the right. We decided that he knew what he was doing and followed him around the bend. It looked very shallow in places but we managed to get through and anchored up alongside the veggie boat after the Westerly Corsair Fair Encounter was leaving a free space (it was very crowded and very little parking).

We took the dinghy over to Alvor Town which was populated by local Brits and all the shopkeepers were English. After a quick view of the town we returned promptly to the boat as the tide was on the ebb and our earlier experience was still very fresh in our minds.

In a matter of less than two hours the channel had already shrunk drastically and we had difficulty spotting a suitable exit. But we managed and then just before turning left to leave the harbour bay entrance we saw a boat stranded and lying at an angle out on the exact place we nearly got stuck coming in. It was Fair Encounter!

I radioed them on the VHF and heard the very strained and nervous voice of John. He had launched his dinghy and off loaded his heavy gear. There was little we could do as we would have got stuck as well. I impressed on John to contact me if there was anything I could help with. In the panic situation I don't think he really registered my concern to help. Perhaps he was keen to get out of his predicament on his own?

We carried on and once again nearly grounded on the final entrance Bar. Not something I want to repeat again if I ever come to Alvor.

New Friends in Lagos

That night we met up with Adrian, a friend from the UK who keeps his boat permanently moored in Lagos. He was a fellow sufferer of the old story where one of a partnership are really set on living and sailing on their boat but the other partner pays lip service to what appears to be a beautiful dream. But then the crunch comes and the partner pulls out with drastic results. Adrian kept a happy and positive attitude to this dilemma and I admire him for his resilience. He spent the previous summer on his own but being very gregarious had quickly mixed in with all the expats. Some of which I met that night. Still worried about Fair Encounter I asked the group if he would be OK. They responded positively saying the prevailing high pressure system would increase the tide height. I called John on channel 77 the next day. They had managed to get off but then proceeded to get stuck again on the other side of the harbour channel! So altogether they were stranded for 24 hours.

July 1st 2009. Woke with rather a sore head as we had spent Marcus's last night in Lagos Town. Now I was alone. The local windsurf centre had

agreed to store my equipment for a couple of weeks so off I went to the beach and managed a session. Despite an off shore wind and too
small a sail I quite enjoyed being on the beach and alone for the first time since May 21st.

I wondered how I would manage on my own for three weeks until Diane joined me. I thought about Adrian and the local Brits and joining them but Adrian was expecting his once yearly crew before sailing off. Being on my own reminded me of my brother living in Gibraltar and getting in with the expats. For him it was a disaster with all the drinking, and loneliness that seems to prevail in such confined environments. I wasn't about to fall into that trap. I want to do as the locals do not as the expats do which is typically very English.

3rd July Assisted boat next door. It looked like a brand new Bavaria. The owner was a beginner and struggled to come alongside. He was Portuguese and spoke decent English. I offered to help him improve his mooring skills. It's now my 3rd night staying in. Too tired, what with the windsurfing and the sun is getting hotter. I'm not complaining though. Get up in the morning, nice breakfast in the morning sun, bit of Spanish lessons, shopping then on the beach for another windsurfing session. Followed up by a nice espresso coffee on the way back to the boat. Then a nice cool beer and dinner cooked to my own satisfaction. This is the life I thought.

Make the best of it as I already know that sailing is all ups and downs and there's sure to be a low just around the corner.

4th July. The Portuguese family took up my offer and so we went out for a sail. It was the first time they had put up the sails. I was very proud knowing I could show them all the basics. Quite an old seadog. Nuno's family was so friendly. Both he and his wife are Doctors based in Lisbon and the boat is the fulfillment of a lifelong dream. Their children are very bright and obviously take after their parents who seem to be typical of the Portuguese middle class elite.

Met Adrian and his crew in the Marina South Bar together with the expats. Quite a gathering. Finished the day with a Piri Piri in an Irish Bar. Charged 20 euros for a bit of Chicken soaked in Piri Piri Sauce. No wonder I prefer eating in on the boat. Evening ended up with Adrian's nephew falling in love with at girl selling the delights of a local bar behind the main town drag. As expected when we went in there was nobody else there except us.

The next night I met up with Adrian and his friend and daughter from Doncaster. A genuinely nice guy. The restaurant purported to be the oldest in Lagos so they charged more for very average wine and food. I returned to the boat feeling a bit "beered out". The next day the Portuguese family turned up and presented me with some lovely presents as a thank you for the sailing support. There was special Portuguese liquor, a fig and almond cake and a jar of very rich jam made of tomato and cinnamon. Very authentic and a lovely gesture. I was taking to this family and such a strong contrast to the British beer swilling expats.

The next day I forgot to contact Fair Encounter on the SSB Radio. Doubt whether I could have got hold of them. I am quickly losing faith with the SSB set up. Especially as the best recommended book – idiots guide to SSB radio- was listed as £50 on Amazon.

There's been no wind for 6 days so I went to the marina swimming pool only to be told as a boat owner I am not entitled to free use of the pool and needed to get a year's membership for 300 Euros, so off to the beach for a swim. It was cold; too cold.

So each day was set as morning for boat jobs, Spanish revision and afternoon for relaxing and chilling out which invariably meant swimming or windsurfing. All under a warm sun and blue skies. Lovely, jubbly.

Nuno gave me a few oysters and a bit of fish. He has an old friend in Portamao with a fishing boat and took Nuno out for a day. The next day Nuno collected me to pick up Diane from Faro Airport. He gave me a map of Portugal and marked all the best sights to see. We took a quick detour to go through a little town just north of Lagos called Silves, Its one of his favourite places with an old castle and church. Presumably at one time it must have been a prominent port because the river flows through to Portamao. How can I return such hospitality? Such a nice guy.

Here comes Diane

It's Sunday 12th July and Diane's first day in Lagos. I was surprised that she didn't want to stay in a hotel. We spent the day food shopping and seeing Lagos town.

On Monday Diane went on her clothes shopping and exploring trip. I went swimming on the beach and ended up with a dickey back. Must be getting old. Laptop also getting old as it's playing up.

Two expats Doris and Ron were very interested in renting the Fuertaventura apartment. I wondered why they wanted to do this when they have warm sunshine in Lagos. I suppose they wanted a change. They wanted me to fix flights for them. I couldn't believe their cheek. Luckily they never pursued the holiday any further.

The beaches were beginning to get busier due to the summer holidays. Not my cup of tea. Bought a Sarong after seeing Roger wear one on the Portugal rally. They are really comfortable and airy.

Went for a run along the beach to Alvor. I noticed they had at last added some channel markers so it must be a seasonal thing. On the way back I discovered the Fish market. Not impressed. Most of the fish was imported and farmed. Returned to have a swim in the Marina Pool and was stopped and questioned about my card. Found out at last.

It was now Saturday 18th July and each day was mostly spent on the beach, bit of a beer, bit of shopping. Where do the days go to?

So on the Sunday I pumped up the dinghy and took Diane on a tour of the Grotto where we saw Nuno and his family anchored off the beach. The swell was minimal so Diane was excused the wet until a grotto tour boat sped by. The summer season is with us.

Monday 20th July. Set off for Portamao with Diane. There was a big swell and Diane was very sick. I felt quite guilty and really cared for her.

Managed to get to Portamao and anchored off Ferragudo but began to slip so reset the anchor. The next day Diane was much better so we toured Ferragudo. Lovely old town with shops and restaurant. We returned in the evening and ate on the dockside. What a rip off. £65 for two persons. The pilot book had warned us.

We stayed an extra night and tried to set off the next morning except the boat wouldn't move. We were snagged on another bouy. I was just about to get the dinghy out to release the anchor chain when a dinghy arrived from Ferrugo. He released the chain and told me off for anchoring so close to the bouys. Flipping cheek. Arrived back in Lagos with Diane not seasick thank goodness. This journey was very flat with no waves so perhaps she felt less bothered?

The sea water is rapidly getting warmer or am I getting used to it. Whatever it's a blessing as I cannot use the swimming pool anymore as they refused to budge on the £300 per boat charge. I would rather freeze in the sea.

Its 25th July my birthday. Lovely cards from all the family especially the words on Diane's card. Went for an Indian meal in Lagos. How English. Getting a bit maudling and low as Diane's leaving for the UK tomorrow. Wonder how she enjoyed staying on the boat for two weeks? Took Diane back to the airport on Sunday. The local train departs from the marina. Very handy. Had no time to say goodbye at the airport as I had two minutes to get the bus to the train station. It was better this way.

Returned to the boat to meet Marcus and his daughter and son who were joining us for nearly a month.

Sailing holiday with Marcus and his two children

Tuesday 28th July set sail for Portamao. Nice smooth trip so good for the kids and they didn't seem at all affected by sea sickness. A good sign. Anchored off Portamao for the third time. Had another strange dream about not getting my sales quota at work. So I am starting to diarise them. Next day set off for Faro with overnight sail saw loads of dolphins before we anchored off a small island near Ohloa called Calutta. A beautiful place with no cars just tractors to move the sand and goods around.

We decided to try and get as far along the Spanish coast as possible so we set off for an 80 mile trip to Cadiz. The climate was very hot and I wasn't getting much sleep. Perhaps this is why I felt irritable and negative about everything. Most out of character. Made Cadiz in 16 hours with a good sail and sighting of a small 6 foot shark. I sensed the kids were bored with the long monotonous journey.

We moored in Puerto Sherry as all the other marinas were full or reserved for a local Regatta. This marina is a bit concrety but lovely parks along the beach. We walked for miles trying to find Old Town of Santa Maria. We gave up and returned to the boat.

Next stop was Puerto America across Cadiz Bay and close to the Old Town of Cadiz.

Very few tourists and picturesque parks and Cathedral.

I'm sure this was the area that Diane and I visited by car when we toured the Costa Luz a couple of years before. Couldn't find a Tapas Bar for love nor money.

Marcus was getting frustrated because there were no supermarkets around. What we didn't realize was the Spanish opening times. All we had to do was wait until the evening when everything opens and the shops come alive.

2nd August. Set sail for Cabo Roche. The original plan to visit Morocco and Gibraltar had been abandoned since the kids were bored with long passages. I was a bit disappointed but not too unhappy as we had good weather and other places to see.

Anchored off Conil Puerto Bay outside of harbour as it was too shallow inside. From here we could see Cape Trafalgar and Morocco 35 miles away. This was the furthest east we would go and the next morning we returned to Sancti Petri.

A beautiful river inlet that used to be a thriving Tuna fishing port. Sadly nowadays the fish have all been caught and the industry all along this coast has died. The port and houses were almost ghost like as no one lives there anymore.

We had trouble finding a mooring buoy and settled on this rather large commercial buoy. I should have known it would be trouble. Marcus took the dinghy and no sooner had he left when the local ferry returned to moor up. Get off our mooring they shouted in Spanish. I tried to explain I needed

Marcus back on the boat. Eventually after some stressful minutes he turned up and we managed to move further up the river onto a suitable buoy.

Marcus was unable to read the bus times to get to the main town so everyone was frustrated and wanted to return to Cadiz. Kenny said I was outvoted. Little did he know about the rules as I was skipper and owner. We stayed in Sancti Petri I found out the bus times and we stocked up with food at last.

Marcus and his kids took the dinghy across to the beach and went shell collecting. I was rather surprised that children aged 16 and 15 collected shells.

Then I realized how strict and overpowering Marcus was with his kids. They were similar in maturity to my kids when they were 12 to 13 years old. He doted over them too much in my opinion. But perhaps children are protected to this extreme these days.

I went for a run along the beach and noticed the dinghies were being pushed out to sea and fortunately they had at least two rescue boats to tow them back up the river. It was dawning on me how strong a current these rivers have along this coast line.

Wednesday 5th Aug. Sailed back up the coast to Cadiz Bay. We wanted to visit Rota Marina on the north side of the Bay but the local Regatta was still on so all berths were taken. This Regatta was becoming a real pain. We anchored up and took the dinghy. Marcus tried to find a supermarket with no luck and was getting very upset. They went off to have a swim on the beach. It was absolutely packed with tourists so I went off exploring and by early evening all the shops started to open. I bought the provisions and returned to meet the others. I was their shopping hero. I was also concerned about the depth under our anchorage so we returned to the boat. My concerns were justified as there was 2 hours still to go to low water and the depth showed 2.7 metres where we would have grounded. I was put out by the fact that we had to leave Rota. The town looked very interesting with lots of old Arabic buildings and a Fiesta due that evening.

The next day we motor sailed across the Cadiz Bay back to Puerto America marina. I spent a very pleasant evening in Cadiz Old town in a bar which specialized in a local cheese and ham. They had a lot of pictures and a book on very famous matadors including one named Miguelen. The bar man took time to explain his history to me in a very broken English translation.

For some reason we returned once again to the North side of the Bay to Puerto Sherry Bay and anchored off, presumably to save mooring fees. The windlass got stuck and after much banging and swearing we managed to free it. Soon afterwards a chap came across for a chat. He had just sailed from Martinique and lost his rudder 400 miles from the Azores. I must admire his ingenuity managing to steer with no rudder. He explained that he was a part time Salvage Contractor so was well versed in making innovative solutions when needed. He hinted that his 42 foot boat was an abandoned boat so it cost him virtually nothing to buy. Then I remembered seeing him earlier in the day anchored out in the middle of the Bay hanging off the stern, I thought it rather strange at the time but that's sailing for you. He was quite confident he could get another rudder for a few euros in Cadiz. This is where we differ so much. I would have had to spend thousands getting a new rudder.

Visit to Sevilla

On the Saturday I set off to Sevilla by train from Cadiz. I had thought seriously about visiting the Town by boat but it entailed at least 8 hours motoring up the River Guadalquiver. The train ride went through very flat and boring countryside so the boat trip would have been very unexciting.
Sevilla boasts the biggest cathedral in the world. Its name is Giralda and is mentioned in the Guinness book of records. It was certainly impressive and held the tomb of Christopher Columbus. The town is very large and it took a lot of walking to see the other museums. Altogether a very worthwhile visit. Pity I lost my pictures from the camera,
Off once again to try and moor in Rota but still full up so we carried on to the River Guadalquiver entrance to berth in Chipiona marina. Before we left I told marina security in Puerto America that our friend with the broken rudder had parked his dinghy alongside our boat and hotfooted off to meet his family in Cadiz. They were not amused because we were leaving and the dinghy was a security threat. They wanted to escalate the situation. Whilst they argued amongst themselves we quietly left. They didn't chase after us.
When we reached Guadalquiver there was a 2 knot flood tide on the go. We couldn't find a suitable mooring off a place named Bonanza so motored further up and anchored off a national heritage area.

That evening I happened to spot a herd of wild pigs running along the beach and a herd of cattle. Very interesting but I was concerned with the strength of the current and at around 11pm we noticed the boat had slipped a bit. The river would only have taken us out to sea if it did get worse so we decided to stay put. Not a very good night's sleep. The following morning I was awakened by a loud chorus of singing birds. There must have been at least 200 swallows perched on the mast and spars.

Apart from the anchor problem a very pleasant stay. So peaceful.

We took the boat down the river to Chipiona. Back to civilization with continuous barking dogs. Went for a swim on the beach but so crowded. The town wasn't much better with throngs of holiday makers. Seemed like Blackpool.

Tuesday 11th Aug set sail for Mazagon. Lovely sail across part of wide bay. Bit of bother with bugs, dragonflies and flies but must have been an off shore wind to get them this far out from the coast. Had a nice day relaxing in Mazagon. Another nice sail to River Umbria the next day and anchored up with two anchors just to be sure. But current not as bad as predicted in pilotage book. Took time out from relaxing to clean the hull. Noticed the anti-foul degrading nothing too serious but must be down to warm waters here. Also cleared the speed wheel by pulling out the plug. This was the first time I had done this exercise and felt very unsure about opening a hole through the underneath of the boat. But it was relatively simple with very little water coming through in between plugging the hole. Cleaned the wheel and returned to seating in hull.

Meanwhile Kenny and Jessica had gone shopping in Umbra and bought me a replacement Coffee cafeteria. It was nice surprise.

Our next destination was only 4 miles away but it had a very tricky entrance. El Rompido was a lagoon just on the other side of the Umbria River. We arrived near the channel approach and watched a few boats leaving. It was strange to see them sail along the coast disappear behind a promontory and then appear again on the other side.

We waited a couple of hours to high tide and then started to enter. It was a challenging entrance but had a minimum of 2.7 metres under the hull. The town was my favourite so far. It was small, clean and very friendly. Just a very nice atmosphere. A place I could live except for the long distance to get in and out of the lagoon.

We had a problem releasing the second anchor but managed to use the windlass and then set off down the lagoon to anchor nearer the entrance. Here it was more commercialized but ideal for water sports. I was hoping to do a bit of windsurfing but the wind didn't get up until later in the evening and then there were too many boats around. By bedtime we were encircled by a dozen motor launches that had decided to have a get together for a night of fishing. Rather noisy but it was Friday night after all

Saturday 15th August. Off to Ayamonte which is on a river separating Portugal and Spain. There are two marinas on the river. We chose the Spanish marina Ayamonte. It was very hot and the nearest beach was 6 miles away so I tried the river beach which was not very nice but cool. That night I found a Tapas Bar that sold my favourite food Albondigas which is meatballs in a sauce. Yum yum. It was so odd to see young girls out on the town wearing jeans in at least 28 degrees. Yet in England the girls wear the skimpiest of clothes in freezing cold winter. Youth is so strange sometimes.

In keeping with the ups and downs of sailing this perfect day turned out to be a very sad day. Barbara rang me to tell me that her husband Robin had passed away at the age of 55 after a repeat of his bowel cancer. Robin had sailed on DwW before I left England and then he was undergoing surgery but did manage to sail with us. It was his love and I can only hope it gave them both some enjoyment in his last months.

Tavira was our next stop. On the way we came across a massive stream of fish extending at least 2 miles long. They looked suspiciously like mullet and they were. Perhaps they were feeding on an outfall from somewhere. We tried feeding them bread but they were not interested. The food they had from the possible outfall must have been good.

We anchored up in the estuary which had a strong current. Par for the course I suppose. It was a very nice river with very few houses and access to beaches both on the river side and a short walk over to the sea side. It was a very popular place for touring boats. We anchored on one buoy but instinct told me it was a private buoy, sure enough, because later on a catamaran arrived gesticulating to us in a friendly way. We knew very well his motives so we promptly moved over to another buoy and watched him moor up with a very nice young lady. An hour later he came across with his dinghy and gave us a nice bottle of wine. I guess he must get a lot of boats arguing about his buoy at this time of year and it must have been nice for a boat to move off without any bother.

Sunday Aug 17th. From Tavire we headed back to Ohloa and Calatra. Another windless and very hot day. Well into the 30's so a swim on Culatra beach was a welcome respite. This must be the best beach around and very little used.

Stopped off in the village to have a meal and Marcus was charged 8 Euros for his kid's chips.

Marcus is not one to discuss disputes quietly so there was a commotion with the waitress. This was the second incident of over charging. Perhaps we had been unlucky or perhaps the Portuguese restaurants take advantage in the summer season.

Wed 19th Aug. Long trip back to Lagos.

Felt that it was going to be hard to adjust to a busy Marina with lots of people and facilities. I had been sailing around on the boat for nearly four weeks. This gave me a real sense of independence and quiet happiness not having to deal with other people and places and stress. The wild life and remote river inlets were never far away from big towns yet offered a complete contrast especially as it was the middle of the school holidays. A strange phenomenon. I'm sure Marcus enjoyed having the company of his kids for a whole month. At home they live with their mother in Southend and Marcus lives in Marlow. Each weekend he picks up his children and returns them on the Sunday. A round trip of 350 miles every weekend. A dedicated Father indeed. Did they enjoy the holiday? I think they will look back in time and say it was a good adventure.

Back in Lagos

Friday 21st Aug. Nose to the grindstone due to lots of work required on the boat including a full service for the engine. Picked up parts for the transom support and various other bits. It cost me 200 euros. They are so expensive but very handy to have nearby.

Met up with Adrian again, who is a happy fellow despite his divorce. I respect such positiveness. I cannot abide people with a chip on their shoulder who think the world owe them something. He said he wanted to meet a good looking woman who enjoyed sailing, intelligent and loads of money. He had high expectations for a 50+ divorcee. I replied saying "get real have you seen yourself in the mirror recently". It was meant as a joke and he took it as such. That's what friends are for isn't it?

Adrian hasn't stopped retelling the joke since. Perhaps it had a ring to it.

I was beginning to get into the Lagos routine. Work on the boat in the morning; go shopping then onto the beach for windsurfing followed by a nice cup of coffee on the way back. What a delightful life. One night I went to a Fado performance in the main Lagos theatre. The audience looked very well turned out and seemed to know each other. Could be the Lagos landed gentry. The singing was very professional but not as good as the impromptu setting in Nazare which was much more fun. Fell asleep during part of the performance. A Sign of old age or perhaps just relaxed. Certainly wasn't through tiredness since the days were getting cooler and sleep was good.

One day I was on the beach and it was very windy and rough. This created a strong eddy on the beach which was great fun to swim around. In the background I could hear this whistle blowing. It was the lifeguard shouting at me to get away. "You are a nuisance, do as you are told; you are setting a bad example". Apparently I did not react quickly enough for his liking. He started jumping up and down, shouting and threatening to call the police. I think he was very serious so off I went with my tail between my legs.

Monday 24th August. Over the road from the Marina were three or four old chimneys still standing and a favourite stack for the nesting Herons. This day I noticed they had gone. Where to I wonder? The season was moving on. A brand new 46 foot Island Packet yacht arrives with 6 lovely young girls on board. Perhaps I should let Adrian know. Perhaps he would have a heart attack. Better not.

Met a new neighbour Martin. He lives here on the boat but plans to move back to Scotland. He misses the summer midgets and the cold winters. He was trying to be serious. We took quite a liking to each other as we shared very similar views such as why did the government bail out the rich bankers? Politicians are a waste of time and what have they done to our pensions. He gave me a full copy of CMap covering the world. Quite a saving. This week there are two funerals. Robin is being buried at sea just off Shoreham. There is a special area preserved for such occasions. Dan a friend of Matthew and Jamie has died from Cancer. He was in his early thirties and married with a child. Such a desperate loss at such an early age.

One night I was just going to bed when I heard some excellent rock music coming from the other side of the bridge. I quickly got dressed and headed over to a small café by the garage and there was this band just packing up. Shame - they sounded very good. They promised to return the next evening and so they were. I sat there for a good hour with just a few café clients. It was a good evening of music with no audience as such to distract from the superb rock music.

With so much time to myself and a determination to keep costs down (despite rip off boat running costs) I was eating in almost every night. My cooking proficiency was coming on leaps and bounds. I cooked my first spagbol and it wasn't half bad. Second helpings please.

Diane rang and reported on her night with an Anne Summers gathering. I chuckled and mentioned Dildos and things. She was not at all impressed. But what do Anne Summers offer apart from fun sex? I treat all this with laughter. It's all good innocent fun.

Time to go shopping for boat things again. This time I am going to find an ironmonger which should be a lot cheaper than the Marina Chandlers. After much walking I found the place and bought heavy duty hammer, jemmy and hacksaw blades. Hopefully such heavy duty tools will never be used.

I was beginning to chat with Martin quite regularly. He actually lives in Lagos with his girlfriend Hillary who was trying to find a new life after selling her Michelin Star restaurant in Edinburgh. She met Martin in

Scotland and followed him out to Lagos and bought a quaint little one up one down in Lagos centre next to the castle.

Her cooking was absolutely delicious as I found out one night when they invited me to dinner. Very nice. Quite strange staying in a house sitting in an easy chair with no rocking motion of the boat albeit only for a few hours.

The next day I went for a very long run to Alvor entrance and back. I was knackered and should have stayed on the boat that evening. However went for a meal with Graeme instead of resting.

Sure enough the weakest point on my body reacted and piles developed. Unfortunately it was a Sunday and I couldn't buy the best remedy which is frozen peas and a bag of ice cubes. The pain was not very nice and I also had a bad cold developing. Managed to buy the necessary cure the next day and periodically sat around on my bag of ice and frozen peas. Not a moment to be shared with friends but very effective.

By the Tuesday the piles were on the descendent and the wind was good, so not to miss out I took some Ibuprofen and had the best days windsurfing. On the downside I left a towel and book somewhere around the windsurfing centre and never found them again. Very odd why would someone want these two items.

It was the end of August. The firework display sparked off the end of the summer season. All the fun banana boats and pedaloes were being stored away and the beaches now almost deserted. One of the beach assistants was walking around with a chameleon on his back and I spotted two on the beach.

Perhaps it was the change in weather that kept my ailments hanging around. Chesty cough and cold, back felt very dodgy but I was determined to make the best of the remaining windsurfing days. I'm a fool. Martin was about to return to Scotland and his family for a couple of weeks. Hilary was also returning. Quite extraordinary relationship going on here. Not my business. Everyone to their own.

It was at this time I met an American delivery skipper named Glenn who was also into windsurfing. He was looking after a 55 foot Discovery and awaiting the arrival of the owner. I joined him for cocktails so he could tell me about the Caribbean and his favourite spot which was The Bitter End in the BVI's. What a boat. Brand new with all the gizmos. He gave me a really cold beer and served olives and bits. Two fridges, microwave oven. What luxury. Then he described various parts of the Caribbean the islands that we should visit and so on. I was getting very excited and looking forward to realizing my dream.

Nuno and family returned for another holiday, they had managed to find a cafeteria coffee maker in Lisbon. Fantastic surprise.

Spoke with Diane. She was concerned with Carol our sister in law who was looking after her poorly Mum and moving house. Its times like these that women are vulnerable and Carol missed having Mike around to share the burden. That's life I guess. Back home it was getting cold and wet. I was here enjoying the blue skies, warm sunshine and my own company. I must be very sad, the last time I was away any length of time on my own goes back to when I lived in a flat in London. Then a weekend alone seemed a long time. Yet here I was two weeks on my own and enjoying every minute. It cannot last.

Glenn came over and had a look at the SSB. He managed to tune into BBC Radio but it was too busy to get any weather signals in the marina.

Tuesday 8th -21st Sept. Decided to return to the UK. Nothing changed really. Much colder and dull skies. Funny how I had adapted to living on the boat. Didn't want to listen to the news and Diane and Matthew were going about their daily business as though I wasn't there. Felt a bit out of it actually. Visited the Southampton Boat Show and stocked up with a load of kit mostly electronic stuff. Couldn't believe how much I had ordered and purchased over the net. It took my whole weight allowance for baggage.

22nd Sept. Back in Lagos with the sun on my back. It's only 8 degrees warmer but feels so much better. The fridge had broken but a local guy replaced the condenser and a reasonable price to boot.

My Brother joined me on the boat. He looked well and in good spirits. It had been a long time since we spent time with each other. Having seen the loss of our two brothers we definitely shared a special fondness for each other. I felt Terry took on too much. All his children, the youngest 18 were still living at home and he paid all their living costs including cars, insurance, and dentist bills. No wonder he never had time for himself. I admire his generosity and loyalty to his children. We spent the first day on the beach and as I swam out I saw a fin swimming slowly towards me. It didn't look that big but I wasn't about to go and have a look! By the time I had hotfooted it back to shore it had disappeared.Phew!

Another dinghy disaster

Took Terry out on the dinghy to tour the Grotto caves. On our way back we stopped off just in the river entrance on a small beach. When it was time to return I couldn't start the outboard engine so we started to row up the river to the marina. On the way a yacht offered to tow us back. Reluctantly I accepted (somehow a sixth sense was nagging me not to accept) but we did and as we approached the Bridge the skipper panicked and rushed forward to get through the open bridge. The sudden acceleration caused the dinghy to overturn and throw us into the river. By the time I came up to the surface and regained my presence of mind the yacht had scampered off through the bridge still with the dinghy on tow!

I couldn't see the outboard engine on the back so assumed it had sunk together with our belongings. We had capsized very close to the waiting pontoon so were able to swim over to it. I quickly run to the marina office and realizing our dilemma they asked if I wanted a diver to rescue our stuff. Yes I said. It took at least 30 minutes for him to dive as he wanted a look out boat to ward off any yachts coming up the river. He searched and searched for 45 minutes without finding anything. By now we had come to the conclusion that all our belongings had sunk and drifting down the river.

Terry lost his watch, camera, mobile, wallet and gold bracelet. I lost my camera, wallet and mobile. We were so annoyed. Why didn't the skipper wait to see if we were OK? It's the first law of sailing.

By now the diver had got dressed and presented me with a 75 euro bill for his services and the marina duty officer had received a message from the yacht owner confirming the dinghy was available for collection on the hammerhead pontoon D. The lookout boat kindly offered to take us there and as we approached I saw to my amazement the outboard engine on the dinghy. Also there was still one bag remaining which was mine. So I still had a mobile and credit cards but my camera was well and truly knackered. Terry didn't recover his stuff.

Graeme kindly offered to take me to a friend's villa on the outskirts of Lagos. John was an engine mechanic and by the afternoon had stripped the outboard engine serviced it and made ready for me to collect. What a relief. Never knew why the damn thing broke down in the first place.

Had a superb evening talking and bonding with Terry. So nice to share memories and similar interests and ideals. We left for Portamao the next day and although Terry doesn't have the slightest interest in sailing he managed very well and wasn't seasick. Another enjoyable stay in Ferrugo and on our return was followed by a rare downpour of rain, thunder and lighting but the worst was far behind us so no real concern.

Sunday 27th Sept. Went for a run and swim in the rain. Martin and Hilary returned from the UK. Martin is a bit of a gizmo and said he bought his GPS and Cmap set up for £35. My Garmin setup was £2500.

Days are drawing in. The Herons are back on their chimney nests. Wonder where they went?

Terry returns home tomorrow. He's been great company and I will miss the opportunity we had to get so close again. It's unlikely we will do such a thing together again. Sad Day.

Tuesday 29th Sept. Electrics Day. Of all the components I bought from the UK the TV monitor was the largest. I bought it second hand and it was the only one that plugged straight into a 12v system. Martin suggested I could wire the monitor straight into the saloon light. Um I thought. Not a good idea. It made a sizzling sound. Monitor had a 2.5 amp reading whilst the light switch obviously had a higher ampage. Took the monitor to the computer repair shop. Didn't expect to see it again. Doh.

Still missing home a lot. Terry had a profound effect. Questions such as mortality, role in life, what am I doing here. Confidence at very low ebb. This has not happened to me many times in my life. Perhaps I have spent too much time here and when we get going again I will be OK. I hope so because there are some very big challenges coming up.

I wonder if Diane has adjusted to a life without me. Perhaps she has no need of me anymore.

Another strange dream. I was a cosmonaut in deep space - very real - great views of the stars and planets. I often dream of flying from building to building. Just flap my arms and off I go. What a lovely feeling.

Enough of the maudling it's better if I get on with working and domestics on the boat. Surprising how good it was just to be busy with simple jobs. Derek of Andiamo came for a chat. He bought a water osmosis system in the UK costing only £160 and swears by it.

"Water tastes as sweet as nectar," he said"

Teddy Bears Picnic.

Martin and Hilary picked me up for a day in the countryside. We headed off for Barregem Resevior. On the way we picked wild figs and pomegranates. Also a small round orange/red fruit with a pimply skin. Very tasty.

The reservoir was enormous. We walked around to the other side and parked ourselves by the waters edge. It was very strange not to swim in salty sea water. I noticed there were no birds singing or signs of wildlife. A lovely relaxing day with two very well informed and charming people. I could get to know them lots more as close friends.

Let it all hang out - decided to run along the beach to Alvor and have a swim. That end of the beach is very secluded and a recognized nudist spot. Let's give it a try. So off with the trunks. What a refreshing difference. Free and easy with the sun on my back and all over. I felt a bit embarrassed but what the hell, it was so invigorating after my recent low days.

Fair Encounter returned from their Mediterranean trip so we all went for a meal that evening. They are completing exactly the same journey as me and returning with ARC Europe next year so we have a sort of affinity with each other. Well that's how I feel but over dinner I'm not sure John and Joyce have the same thoughts. Perhaps they think I am a bit of an amateur since they have completed many more years sailing than me. Also they are a lot more knowledgeable and technically qualified. Joyce knows everything.

My faithful Crew

Saturday 3rd Sept. My final guests arrive for a week's holiday. Gill, Matt and Dave are original crew founders who joined me as new starters in 2007 so we already had a fond regard for each other. Dave had just separated from his wife of 25 years and was still getting used to his bachelor status. His friend Clive the fireman accompanied him.

Gill was as chirpy and chatty as ever whilst Matt quietly stands by. Gill insisted on carrying her own enormous suitcase. A smashing pair ideally suited for each other.

All headed for the swimming pool. I was a little reticent but the summer holidaymakers were now all back home so the pool attendant turned a blind eye to the yachties using the pool. That evening we walked over the bridge to the busiest and most popular restaurant in Lagos. Nothing special but the food is good value. We all laughed at the restaurant's music. Some elderly guy playing an electric organ using music by numbers on the keys.

Sunday 4th Sept. Sailed to Albufeira unmistakable with its Lego land painted houses. Glad I didn't stay here for the summer. Soulless place. Should have taken taxi to main Town.

On the way to Ohloa I tried to contact Fair Encounter by SSB Radio, No joy at all, so frustrating.

Clive was a laugh a minute with some great jokes about the fire brigade. Stories of things they get up to whilst awaiting the call. One such practical joke involved a look-alike rat on the end of a piece of string which they would string out along the pavement from the office window. He insisted that after pub closing time when couples came along it was always the girl that would chase the rat whilst the bloke looked on.

We were in fits of laughter. It's definitely the way you tell them.

We stopped over for a night in Culatra and spent a day on the deserted beach followed by lunch. I didn't have to ask them if they were enjoying themselves. It was a long way from the stress of work at home.

On to Vilamora and arrived at 19.30 just in time for berthing. I had heard that the Marina was quite up market. It was full of massive Gin Palaces a Rich man's heaven. It's also very popular with the golfing fraternity so all the bars and restaurants were lively.

On the way back we were followed by thunder, lightning and hailstones but an excellent sail to Portamao. Here we moored up in the Marina and met a fellow Westerly Oceanranger owner. He and his partner had retired from the forces and were living aboard. The boat was in immaculate condition.

Whilst we saw them he was busy polishing and scrubbing. He had sailed all his life and it looked as though he could handle any sailing challenges with little difficulty. He predicted we would complete the ARC in 20 days. I hope he is right. Met up with Adrian's friend Graeme who had also sailed into Portamao that night on his Sunbeam yacht Duke's Dream. A beautiful if not well known make from Austria.

A Drawbridge too far

What a lovely morning on Portamao Beach, before a great sail back to Lagos. As we approached the drawbridge another boat suddenly left the visitors mooring and shoved in front of us to pass through the open bridge. By the time we followed them in the bridge started to close very quickly. A very swift about turn saved us a rather nasty situation. I radioed the marina office but they waffled on not giving a satisfactory answer as to why we had nearly been squashed. I know now that the yacht that shot in front of us must not have spoken on the VHF and was assumed to be the only yacht going through.

Every cloud has a silver lining and the next incident was a positive one. In Lagos they have a daily radio station called Navigators Net. Pity I didn't find out sooner about this very useful facility. I put in a request to ask if anyone knew about SSB Radio. Bingo. Mike of Kelly's Eye came around and suggested I use a certain channel. Back he went and soon we were chatting loudly to each other. I was so pleased.

It's now the last day of the crews holiday we had a great tapas meal to send off what was a wonderful and enjoyable week with good friends. "Just can't get enough" Dave, "Chirpy" Gill and "Quiet" Matt and "Fish Pie" Clive. Really hope Dave will soon find a good girl to fill his life. He deserves it despite being a Man Utd fan.

Saddle Up

My routine of late includes a visit to the windsurfing and then a bike trip further along to the naturist beach (sounds better that nudist beach). I locked up the bike in a small village by the beach. It looked a bit seedy and true to form when I returned they had stolen my saddle. Bloody thieves. Should have known better than leave something in a dodgy area.
I spoke with Martin about the missing saddle and Hilary took me to a local cycle repair centre. The standard saddle fitting was too narrow so they spent 30 minutes adapting the fitting all for 3 euros.
That evening had a lovely meal at Hilary's house. She certainly proves her Michelin star status.
12th October. Finally completed the boat for passage to Gran Canaria via Madeira. I have done all I can to make the boat ready.
Then a bolt out of the blue -Hilary wants to join us for the Madeira trip.

AAA

Another Alvor Accident. The channel markers are still installed so couldn't understand how boat became grounded. Good day on deserted beach. Did "Chariots of Fire" along beach with no trunks on. Must be the sea air or something. Later that day an expat came up mentioning something about nude man on the beach today. Good on him I said. He obviously knows it's me but I couldn't care a stuff. We're off in a week so it may be the last time I ever do such a thing again.

15th October Tony joined me on the boat. He's completing Step Four to Heaven and flying back to the UK from Gran Canaria in a couple of weeks. Tony is an ex director of a large clothes manufacturer in Nottingham and very well informed and articulate. Also sailed his own boat to the Caribbean so plenty of experience.

Thought I had completed boat readiness but discovered hot water leaking into bilge. Had a go at mending it but had to call in the local engineer, who provided a new water pump for £200. Not bad for these parts.

Just to top off a frustrating day the door of the marina's washing machine had jammed, so another session of getting the staff to open the door as I didn't want to force it open.

Whilst getting shopping with Tony we happened to walk along the upper verandah along the Marina. It was the first time I had ventured past the upstairs Bar so what a surprise when I saw a Tapas Bar with my favourite

Albondigas meat balls advertised, which was so annoying when I have been here for 4 months and never found a decent Tapas Bar in Lagos Town. That's life.

The Last Supper

Nuno and family have invited me to their favourite local fish restaurant in Portamao together with his sister who works at the Oceania Beach Golf Club. They are such a talented family. John is only 6 and already speaking some English. The restaurant was filled with local people and the fish was delicious. They are hoping to visit London in February and Nuno's dream is to sail to The Azores. I shall have to keep in touch with them.

It's now Sunday 18th October and our last few days in Lagos. It feels like the end of a holiday and waiting around to go home. Went out with Adrian on the last night and he took us to this "highly rated" Karaoke Bar. What a bore. Never have been into amateurs trying to be professionals. Oh well Adrian as always full of life and joking. A nice guy.

Whale or optical illusion?

Fourth Step to Heaven – Off to The Canaries

First stop Madeira.

Had a slight delay whilst the engineer fitted the water pump and Marcus arrived from the UK straight off the train. Seems a bit distant to me. Perhaps he was getting used to being back in boat mode and a new crew. Plan is to head south initially as heavy weather expected. No sooner had we left when Hilary became very seasick.

24 hours into our passage and the wind was getting serious. Much stronger than the UGrib predictions of 30 knots. Still heading South towards Africa F9 gusts and Tony sick in the night. Not a good start. Gust of 55 knots just recorded. Tony showed us how to heave to by backing the Genoa opposite to mainsail and then locking off Steering wheel. Ok we would not be able to steer a course but with the nearest land some 200 miles away it wasn't an issue. It certainly worked because the boat instantly flattened and steadied itself. We just sat in the saloon until the worst passed through which happened very shortly.

Two days out and still very confused seas making it very hard to write my diary. The SWesterly wind was pushing us ever further south towards Africa but little we could do with the wind straight on our nose. Hilary still very poorly. Wish the wind would change anywhere but SW. I felt like Scott of the Antarctic. Should never have left Lagos with such a weather system coming in.

Hilary kicks the bucket

After four days Hilary dispenses with the bucket and manages to keep down a bit of melon and ginger biscuit. Still no decent wind and now have engine on. I reckon we got within 100 miles of the African coast near Casablanca. The strong winds have taken their toll and its repair day for me. Doris the Duogen was missing some bolts and Larry the auto helm was suffering from a loose wheel drive. Also needed to fill up fuel tank from spare tanks. Not a simple task in good weather let alone seas with a big swell. It would have helped if I had a long pipe that sucked up the fuel as one does with a car, but not so, I had to struggle with Marcus pouring most of the fuel on my head. My hair has been blond ever since!

Everyone very tired. Worst trip I have experienced and also for Tony with all his sea miles under his belt. The swell was so bad I needed to catch some sleep on a decent bunk because my aft cabin bunk although large and comfortable was not fit for the job when rolling around in heavy seas. Both Marcus and Tony were upstairs on watch and I parked myself alongside Hilary on the double bunk which is much flatter in the middle of the saloon. It didn't seem out of place sharing a bunk with a good looking woman and later I thought of what Hilary was thinking at the time? I will never know. It was nice to get a few winks sleep after the experience we had been through.

The fifth day and the wind has at last changed so we can put up the sails. Only 200 miles to go. The detour has increased our passage from 480 nm's to 600 nm's. We are so far south we will not be able to get up to our planned stopover in Porto Santo which has a wonderful beach and beautiful island. That's sailing I suppose. Tony must have questioned my seamanship skills departing in such weather but he didn't complain. A well seasoned sailor who was such a positive asset to the journey.

It was a much better day and for the first time we could eat on deck and enjoy the 30 odd pod of Dolphins that joined us. I wonder if they visit places at certain times. They do seem to always going or coming from somewhere.

25th October and can see Madeira in the distance. Owing to the extended time at sea the last meal was Pasta which Marcus hates so Hilary cooked him an omelette. The best he had ever eaten. She certainly knows how to cook. Then we were joined by a large pod of Pilot whales just outside of Madeira. Finally arrive in Madeira and have managed to secure a mooring in Funchal Harbour with the help of Diane who was now in Madeira and went to the marina office to ensure we had a mooring since I was unable to raise them on the VHF. Only one beer in fridge so Marcus takes on a big sulk. I wonder if he is regretting signing up for all stages of the trip.

Hopefully the arrival of Mary tomorrow will cheer him up.

Madeira

We planned to stay a week exploring the island. Hilary flew back to Scotland and Tony was happy to explore on his own. Mary and Marcus were booked into a nice hotel in the beach/holiday area. Diane had booked an economy hotel a couple of miles outside of Funchal. It soon dawned on me that getting anywhere in Madeira was a major commitment due to the sheer mountain drop from coast to hinterland.

I said my farewells and left the Marina with Diane to find a restaurant. We did this and then the impact of the last weeks sailing hit me. We found a park nearby and I just completely flaked out. 2 hours later I woke and we returned to the hotel where I slept undisturbed through the night.

There's plenty to see and do in Madeira. We did the ski lift tour up to the tropical gardens. Diane was beginning to panic as we got higher. Funchal has a unique Toboggan Ride from the top of the ski lift. Two men push the armchair, which has wooden runners, down a special street back to Funchal. Looks fun but Diane wasn't that keen.

Tours are very expensive so we tried to walk and bus to various spots including Conico with has a gigantic statue of Christ on the hill. Mochico was a nice quiet seaside town, just a short bus ride from Funchal.

The island tour by coach is worthwhile. At Porto Maniz they have built some giant swimming pools carved out of the rock lava overlooking the sea. In land we saw the original dwelling houses of the inhabitants which are very small. The hillsides have very rich soil but areso steep that the farmer has to chain his cattle to prevent them falling off the edge. The farmer leaves the farmhouse on the top of the hill and lives down the bottom of their land in a shed returning at the weekend.

Everyone who visits Madeira has to go on the Levados Tour. The Levados are very long ditches or small aqueducts that sweep all over the hillside delivering fresh water to the towns. They all have spectacular walks alongside. I was very tempted to have a swim in one of the waterfalls but it was too cold. Diane just loved the greenery and fauna and flora.

Our guide was a young fellow and very well versed on his subject matter. As an aside he recommended we visit the California Hotel restaurant which was opposite our hotel. The steak was prepared on a stone and the best one I have had for a very long time, and at a reasonable cost.

It's the 30th Oct and time for Diane to return to the UK. Once again I felt extremely lonely and lacking in confidence returning to the boat. But not so bad once I started busying myself with jobs. That night we dined on the old Beatles yacht named Vagrant. Even now 30 years on it looked fabulous.

Last night in Madeira and ate in the Marina. The fish was old and dry and the bill extortionate. I don't recommend staying in Funchal. It's a rip-off. Typical tourist take you for a ride town.

My niece Jo Anne from Wolverhampton joined us for the last leg to Gran Canaria. She is a local GP but also gained a PHD in Biology. Very bright and hopefully not above our station.

We had planned to leave on the 2nd November and did in fact depart in the afternoon only to be met by very strong winds. Back we go for a further night in Funchal. Everyone fed up and grumpy. Managed to finally depart the next day and Tony caught our first fish on the boat. It's a very common fish in these parts and is called a Mahi Mahi or Dolphin fish. Just enough for 4 and really tasty. Managed to sail 120 miles with a good wind but beginning to experience heavy Atlantic swells. Not very good for sleeping and by the second night I was lacking substantial sleep. We stopped off at a protected desolate Island called Selvagem (pronounced salveges).

Not a place to be listed high on your favourite places to visit. It's inhabited by a couple of students who volunteer to watch over the natural animals and birds on the Island.

Beautiful seclusion but extremely hard to access. There is just one large mooring buoy that is used for the Ferry boat to deliver provisions. We tried to secure DwW but the swell was very difficult and would cause serious damage to the hull if the weather deterioted. So we gave up the idea of mooring to explore and continued on our way to The Canary Islands.

Here I had a dilemma. I wanted to visit my apartment in Fuertaventura but it was an extra day's sail with wind on the nose. And we had to meet up with the incoming ARC crew. Once again crew's timing issues plagued me. I know it can't be helped because people have commitments and time is always at a premium these days.

Reluctantly I agreed to head to Tenerife instead and next day we moored up in Santa Cruz. I spent all my spare time repairing bits on the boat. I think the Lagos to Gran Canaria stage has taken its toll in both wear and tear of boat and people. On reflection I wonder why I didn't plan to leave Lagos in August/September when we would have had a better chance of fairer weather.

7th Nov. We left Tenerife at 4 am the next day. Tony and Marcus had decided that my lack of sleep was doing nobody any good and could endanger the boat so Marcus made up a board to place on one side of my bunk to stop me rolling around. It was difficult to clamber in and out but with a couple of sails on the other side of the bed prevented me rolling around. Good job.

Once again wind on the nose. I guess it's been over two weeks since we left Lagos and the amount of sailing days can be counted on one hand. But finally we arrive in GC.

Step Four to Heaven completed. Hurrah.

8th Nov. It's the last night for Marcus Joanne and Tony so we eat out in the local Sailor Boy restaurant. It's full of sailors getting ready for the ARC and has a tremendous atmosphere. For some reason Marcus is not very happy. He has to return to the UK as his kids were very upset when he told them he will be in the Caribbean for Xmas. So he's having an early Xmas with his family and then returning to GC for the ARC. He started to complain that I had two Tapas courses and then started on at Jo Anne. That was enough. Although I didn't pick up exactly what he said and it was only a couple of words, there is no way he treats my guests or family in that way. So we have our first upset since knowing each other for two years. He denied being derogatory to Jo Anne so I didn't pursue the matter.

Possibly Marcus felt inferior. She certainly expressed her skills and knowledge in just about every subject we covered although she gave up on her sailing prowess and experience soon after we left Madeira. Jo Anne did say she never suffers from seasickness because she has a damaged ear drum and the usual cause of the dreaded ailment is the ear to brain function. She was right on that count. It was quite an experience to get close to an individual who is expected to cure everyone's ailments and provide miracles. I suppose it could make that individual feel rather important and all knowing? Jo Anne is a lovely niece and I enjoyed her company. I'm thinking she enjoyed the experience more than the journey.

I was feeling in good spirits. We had now come 2000 miles from the UK. Completed 4 stages. I was in true boat living mood and feeling very positive for the coming weeks. It was becoming quite noticeable that unless one lives on a boat permanently it takes time to adjust between the two. It's nothing like a caravan holiday where you return home and don't experience a major change. Living on a boat is a very different mind set and needs a few days to adjust to continuing movement and cramped exposed living conditions.

ARC here we come

Pre Arc preparation

It's the 9th November and The ARC office has opened. Not a lot of activity but safety seminar highlighted a lot more bits to do before DwW gets the thumbs up. Have to add a cockpit speaker so the helmsman can hear Channel 16 on the VHF. I argued that we will not be having the VHF during the night because "off watch" crew will be disturbed. They said we should have VHF turned on 24 hours. I suppose they are right. Larry now fixed after replacing the control unit plug. Asked Yachtfunk, a specialized SSB radio repair company to check out the SSB. They found a number of problems. Firstly the Auto Tuner wasn't plugged in (it must have come out on our way from Lagos). The Antennae cable should not share the same ingress hole as the Duogen and the cable should not be strapped to the backstay. After 350 euros of work all was pronounced fit for the job. We will see. I sent a long mail to Eurotek in the UK saying they should compensate me for work that should have been done in the first place. I never received a reply.

We were moored alongside a number of live aboard boats and next door the guy looked as though he did carpentry work so I went over and asked if I could have a couple of bits of wood which I needed to box in the provisions. He quickly replied in broken English "so you want to take a bit of my home". I got the message loud and clear.

The English Calor Gas bottles are generally not available anywhere abroad. I had managed so far but only because Lagos had a contact for refills. So I now needed to change over to the more popular camping gas set up which meant changing the regulator as well as buying different bottles. On reflection I really regretted not converting to the International Propane bottle set up before leaving England. This decision would have made refilling a non issue instead I have had problems all the way down here and it wasn't about to get any better.

Rob from the ARC office turned up unannounced for the safety and rig inspection. I should have said I wasn't quite ready because I couldn't locate items that he was checking such as bolt cutters and spare tiller spanner. Most embarrassing.

Some good news. I received my original boat registration document that I left in Funchal – thanks to a very helpful WCC assistant named Carmen? Who spoke German, French, Spanish, Italian and came from Portugal.

Despite all the work on the boat I did manage to get down to the beach. Had a massage which was only 5 Euros. Good value so relaxing. It was a really nice change just to relax for a few hours and that night, the 13th Nov, we had the official opening of the ARC held in the Town Hall. It was a spectacular show almost on a par with a good west end musical. A great evening topped off by a further Nomad Fiesta in the town centre.

200, 000 people mostly less than 30 years of age milling around 3 major stages for music performances. All free and fantastic atmosphere.

Rigamortis

Next day the Rigger arrived to inspect the boat. This was a free service from Admiral Insurance so very useful for me and them because they get to know what exactly they are insuring. The Rigger was very impressed with all the prep work we had done. This was very much down to Diarmid's good work checking all the split pins, bottle screws and fixtures. A great guy to have around. All the rigger could find wrong was the Radar dome which had a loose pop rivet which I had known about for some time.

The next ARC event was in the very posh La Palma yacht club. Pity the reception sponsored by Berthon couldn't match the occasion. They tried serving cocktails instead of beer but were obviously short of money because they were very watered down.

ARC into top gear

ARC Parade took place today with 32 countries taking part. Quite a turnout. This was followed by Pedro's Dinghy Race. A good time for all with fancy dress and fighting on the water between boats. Complete chaos but great fun. Wish we had the made the effort.

Penultimate day for repairs. I went up the mast to fix radar dome fitting and dropped the pop gun. Diarmid was extremely stressed being a retired safety inspector and all that. So he took my place but still didn't manage to drill out the old rivet for replacement. I wasn't too concerned because the other 5 rivets were secure and WCC inspection didn't cover this particular fault.

Chris the fireman and his partner Julie arrive. They are very excited and good fun.

Finally passed the inspection test after purchasing a lot more first aid stuff including anti biotic and Chris brought a load of burn treatment stuff that impressed WCC inspectors.

Final Day getting closer. Its the 19th Nov and three days to go. All the crew had taken over the provisioning planning and buying. This was a great weight off my mind and helped me concentrate on other boat matters. Also found Diane's watch that had gone missing since Weymouth. Good find. How is it that items get lost so easily on a boat? Marcus returns from the UK all fired up.

The awesome responsibility was now beginning to dawn on me. I felt there was a definite divide between crew and captain although I had a very easy going approach or maybe I was being a bit paranoid. Other skippers showing surprise at what I had achieved in such a small amount of time didn't help my confidence thinking that maybe I should know a lot more to attempt such an ambitious venture.

The last two days were busy with final touches on the boat. Chris fitted the new regulator to use camping gas whilst I fixed 'Senor Furtado' the foldaway bike to the guardrails. This was a compromise as Marcus was for dumping it. Everyone did an excellent job getting the provisions. The local supermarket was happy to deliver the goods and the boat was very quickly getting full. The water bottles were the biggest challenge. 72 x 5 litre containers but DwW was up for it with plenty of storage cupboards and spaces. The whole of the front cabin was dedicated to food, water and bread, with some 20 odd boxes of pre-baked baguettes. The daily provision requirements had been sorted and stored in large plastic containers for easy access. For our fresh meat Chris and Julie had arranged with the hotel to keep it refrigerated until the day of departure.

Final reception in the Sotovento Club. Had trouble with the speaker system so 'Mr. Burns' the MD of WCC couldn't say all his words. Perhaps not a bad thing. We were standing next to the stage and there was this circle of sailors from one of the racing boats standing next to us. One of them couldn't squeeze in unless he stood slap bang next to me so he kept pushing and pushing against me to join the 'in circle'. I was very close to thumping him. I thought how sad some youngsters can be.

Fifth Step to Heaven – Crossing the Atlantic

First over the line, Gran Canaria

It's the 22nd November and time for the OFF. Everyone so excited and busying themselves and the atmosphere was electric. Chris and Julie arrived with a number of large plastic containers. These were the fresh meat containers that should have been kept in the freezer of the hotel. But manana mode took over and the staff left the meat in a fridge instead. The portions were enormous so we would be feasting for the first few days before it all went off. Today was also Matthews's birthday but I couldn't get hold of him so left a message with Jamie and Cara. The racing boats were first to leave to a very loud blast of music from Don Pedro. They played Jungle Book for Bagheera and lots of different country anthems. It was a very special occasion. We left soon after and were greeted by water cannon and surrounded by at least 250 boats in the Bay. Some were lookers on and one crashed into a competitor causing him to retire. How stupid can people be sometimes? I felt really sorry for him.

We found the start line which was a bit of a challenge in all the commotion. Then the cannon fired. St Lucia here we come.

Monday 23rd Nov. The Rally weatherman was uncertain about the famous NE trade winds coming in for the trip. The pre event weather was not at all consistent and was all over the place. But he didn't have to worry. From the very off we had NE winds on a lovely reach heading more or less where we wanted to go. Let's face it with 2700 miles to go a few degrees off for a few hours won't make much difference. Most of the fleet left us on our Port and headed South to catch the stronger NE trades. We decided to follow a more northerly route keeping to the rhum line as much as possible.

The wind gradually increased to F6 as we followed the Gran Canaria coastline, this was too strong for the twin headsail. The swell was on our stern and I, Diarmid and Chris were all experiencing various degrees of queasiness. Good news on the SSB Radio. I managed to make contact with the fleet.

What a whopper

Tried my hand at fishing since we were hearing of lots of success stories with big fish being caught. After an hour I started to reel in the line. Suddenly it went very tight and a fin appeared on the surface 'boathook and gloves' I shouted as I tried to reel it in. Then the line snapped and the lure flew over my head and hit Marcus on the head. The one that got away. Then we saw the first flying fish and the Dolphins joined us to play.

Time to cook all the mince before it went off. There was enough for three weeks supply. What a performance with the curry sauce. Cooking such a large amount confused me.

Two days out and everyone beginning to get their sealegs.

Once we passed the bottom of GC the wind abated and we hoisted the twin headsail which gave us another knot of speed. Best day yet with 135 miles in 24 hours

Chris spotted a tear in the mainsail very close to the top. I was surprised and disappointed because it was a new sail. Took it down and repaired and noticed the tear was the same horizontal line with a join in the mast just where it furls into the mast. Suspected there must be an obstruction inside catching the sail as it is reefed in. Luckily on the second day we dispensed with the mainsail as the twin headsails were doing a fine job.

Three days out and Marcus catches his first fish with a home made hand reel. If the fish are there it's a simple matter of catching them. If they are not around no matter how good one's equipment it will not make a lot of difference. This proved to be so true throughout my travels. Not sleeping very well due to split shifts and restless leg syndrome. Taking two tablets to ensure they work through split shifts.

Everyone settling into a daily routine. I am kept very busy with maintenance checks especially battery power and things that feed off them. Doris and the single solar panel are more than enough to run fridge in the day and autopilot at night. The tri colour bulb has packed up so the 2 amps that it should take at night is a big saver on power. No one seems in a hurry to go up the mast to replace it. Also having the VHF on at night is too noisy so we also switch it off.

Good morning America

I report in at noon everyday on the SSB Net service. I am also a Net Controller so when it's my rota I have to contact the 10 other boats in our handicap group. This has proved to be very successful and good fun. Firstly I collect all the positions. Then I repeat the weather report that we are sent by email each day from the WCC headquarters. Lastly I open up the session for general chat. The SSB has performed very well so far. After the general broadcast I prepare the email of positions on my PC laptop and ask if anyone on the boat wishes to reply to their emails received earlier with the weather report. All of this can take at least an hour and I am very pleased with the performance with both the Iridium phone, SSB Radio and Mailasail software. Once you get to use it properly and know its idiosyncrasies it works very well using encryption and compression tables for simple high speed transmission.

First week

It's Saturday 28th Nov and we have made 920 miles which is an average of 131 miles per day. That's 11 miles extra each day than I planned for and will get us to St Lucia in 21 days. Well under our target of 23 days. No wonder I never win the day's competition guessing the mileage. I am too conservative.

Minor heart attack on the power supply defect. Doris the Duogen was not generating enough power it has been fine for 7 days. So I lift her out and low and behold there was a plastic bag wrapped around the propeller. Good old Doris. Then the Solar panel started to bleep. Very annoying. It's got its own regulator and as soon as the batteries get low it starts to bleep. Wish I was savvy enough to understand the relation between all the regulators. Haven't got a clue why the battery monitor says one reading and then the solar panel regulator goes on bleeping. Oh well at least we are ok on the power supply and I look forward to fault free days and the last 500 miles.

Why 500 miles I ask. Perhaps it's just a milestone near enough to St Lucia for me to feel I have succeeded

Second Week.

We are still on UTC boat time therefore we will gain 5 hours going west and it's now darker in the morning. Fresh food finally finished on the 8th day out. Little bit of cucumber left. Tried some canned meatballs. Worst I have ever tasted. Ugh.

All crew now working out ETA with 1600 miles to the finish. A pointless exercise. We are all getting into this way of life with a standard routine. Each day goes very quickly but I find the nights very long due to my restless legs and getting too hot. But this is a small price to pay for savoring a lifetime adventure. Though it's strange to be soaking up 25 degrees of sunshine in December when it's cold and wet in England.

Haven't heard from Diane for 4 days. I think she is visiting her ailing father in Norwich.

Looking forward to Wednesday and halfway celebrations but then the wind drops. So on with the engine for the first time.

Marcus catches a good sized Mahi Mahi with his new lure and christens it Posh because I charged him what I paid for it, 12 Euros. Then he had the cheek to try and charge us for the fish. A bit fed up with his continuous baiting for mistakenly drinking his water. He was only joking I suppose. It might be something to do with the lack of wind which is putting us a bit on edge. Still it's really good to celebrate halfway to St Lucia.

The climate is getting quite hot especially as we are in the middle of the Atlantic. We have not set our clocks back 5 hours and remain on GMT so not getting light until 9am.

The Solar panel is only supplying 9 volts which is useless. Decided to call the supplier Barden on the sat phone. "Our panels never breakdown, no moving parts so must be your fault". What a response to get from a customer in the middle of the Atlantic. I'm very unimpressed with their attitude and the fact that they want me to send the unit back before they will replace it. Not looking forward to having to chisel it off the deck.

Friday 4th Dec and a very hot and stormy night and we motored South to avoid lightening.

Big rolling seas and nobody really slept properly. Marcus and I had a heated discussion regarding direction. I was for continuing to head south to pick up the stronger winds whilst Marcus was for keeping to the North and the 270 degree rhum line. In the end I think we were splitting hairs as the wind got up and after 18 hours of engine we were back to good sailing. In a way I am glad we were part of the back markers because we could see the really black clouds up ahead and a continuous night of lightening. This bad storm was reported the next day on the net controller role call. Ocean Lady lost the SSB radio transmission so one of the net controller s in our group was now off the air. Also we were getting more and more miles behind resulting in fewer and fewer boats remaining within radio contact of us.

Third Week

Our next mile stone is 675 miles remaining which is the three quarter Mark. Whoops in a rush I kicked the Autohelm control unit. Although handy to use it's in a very awkward place. Hopefully the gaffer tape will aid the bracket. The unit must be held firm or it starts reading the compass wrongly. The telescopic runner for the mast spinnaker pole is also a problem. The plastic runners have worn through but Marcus has managed to fix something up temporarily. Record day for sailing with 156 miles lopped off our journey. Diarmid gets a bit grumpy when under pressure on deck. Everyone getting a bit bored and tired now and wishing we were in St Lucia.

The list of positions to report getting smaller as boats get further and further apart. It's mainly Fair Encounter and DwD acting as Net Controller and relaying weather reports.

Monday 7th December. 675 miles to go. The Weather report is looking very promising for the final push with North easterlies very consistent. Days are hot and sunny but bad squalls at night. The on watch helmsman has to be on the lookout because the squalls come up very quickly from behind and so the lighter twin headsail has to be furled in or risk getting blown out. So far we have managed but the sail keeps wrapping around the furler. Lots of boats have now finished as we pass the 500 mile Mark. Whisky celebration for me as this is my personal goal achieved. My estimate for finishing on Saturday looking good.

Banged my head as I was reading my Spanish lesson on deck and fell asleep. I think the crew are thinking of buying me a crash helmet because every time I get my Spanish book out I fall asleep after 5 minutes. But apart from a painful knee which must be a result of no physical exercise for two weeks, I am very pleased with everyone's health, that aside it's difficult to get decent sleep in such lumpy seas and hot climate.

Only 80 miles to finish. Diane has already flown in and loves the island.

Saturday 12th Dec.14.12 pm local time. Excellent winds have got us to Rodney bay in 20 days. Fantastic reception. A photographer meets us before the finishing line and takes a great picture of DwW on a broad reach going like the clappers. Lots of motor launches out cheering us over the line and then a warm local reception on the pontoon, with a fruit bowl and of course a Magnum of cold beer. How sweet that tasted. Indeed. DwW got us here safe and sound with minor problems for such an epic journey. Thank you DwW.

Yet with so much success under my belt why did I feel so insecure? Perhaps because we are so far from UK and still have to get the boat back? On reflection I can now say this thinking should have been instantly dispelled and replaced with celebration and enjoyment.

St Lucia

Diane had booked The Ginger Lily Hotel, which was a very good small hotel outside of Rodney Bay but close to the beach. Food and accommodation here is expensive. People very friendly to a point that I wonder if they have another agenda but not so. We get too paranoid in the UK. We should loosen up and take people at face value. Here they are genuinely friendly and interested in you. So refreshing.

Personally for me it took a couple of days to adjust to seeing so many black people and not to compare them to places such as Brixton where one would not venture out at night. But here it truly is their country and they are not out to fleece or mug people. They know very well the consequences for upsetting the island's major earner which is tourists and more tourists.

I blame the media for giving out exaggerated reports about crime here in the Caribbean.

The beach in Rodney bay is very popular and too busy for my liking especially the dreaded sea scooters. It wasn't long before I was swimming on the Gros Islet Bay which is almost empty but access is via the shanty town which is supposed to be off limits for tourists. What nonsense. I'm sure the hotels give out misleading advice because they want their clients to stay in the hotel and eat in the hotel.

The next few days involved a mixture of chilling out on the beach and following up replacement spares, interspersed with ARC get togethers and

Seminars. One seminar was hosted by Chris Boyle who is the authority on sailing around the Caribbean. He's been doing it for 40 years in his catamaran so should know everything there is to know. Afterwards the St Lucia Press wanted an ARC volunteer to appear on their television. Like a fool I let Diane persuade me to speak with them. The next day a shop assistant recognized me from the program on the TV. Whoopee I'm a star.

We did have a few rain showers now and then but generally the weather was warm with blue skies.

Diane and I missed the Rodney Marina sponsored party which spared no expense in entertainment due to it being the first ARC for the incoming Marine manager so his budget was very generous. The wine flowed well, the firework display spectacular and everyone ended up in the swimming pool. The hang over of Marcus and Diarmid certainly backed up the good time reports.

I was very keen to keep costs at a minimum by living on the boat. Diane wasn't having any of it so after the first week we moved into a local cheaper hotel near the Marina rather than the beach. It was very good value for the time of year.

Saturday 19th Sept. It's the closing day and final ARC Party. Lots of prizes to be had. I received a nice bottle of Chairman Rum for my role as Net Controller. Chris and Julie were absolutely plastered. They really are pushing the boat out. Good on them. It's a once in a lifetime event. For my part I retired early with Diane. I think the partying, drinking and celebrating had run its course. Marcus getting itchy feet and wants to move on. I don't blame him as he is on his own. Diarmid returns back to the UK. I wonder what he really thought of the adventure and the rest of the crew. Perhaps I am being too introspective. I'm sure he had a great time. Like all of us.

Visited Pigeon Island the next day. It's a nice walk around the bay and the old Army garrison looks almost as though it was still operative and a soldier would suddenly appear from the gate. I guess the life was very hard for them 300 years ago and they would not have had the same opportunity to chill out on the beaches and just watch the palm trees gently blowing.

Another day with suppliers trying to move spares problems along. It's very apparent that the shops are run by the manager and the assistants are never trained or are incapable of being trained to any level of expertise. So unless one speaks with the manager matters or issues do not get resolved.

Called Chris Barnsfield on the phone to establish his plans to join up for the trip back to the UK. I was a bit concerned that he didn't contact us when he was here in St Lucia after competing the crossing on Fandango another ARC entrant. Perhaps his time was limited. Met Marcus on the boat, he seemed lonely.

We had lunch with Fair Encounter when they returned from the Xmas Boat trip around the Bay. This involved a number of boats dressing up and touring around like a Marde Gra on boats. Not my scene really. A lot of boats had now left the Marina to visit other places for Xmas. So things were very quiet after the recent celebrations.

Sailed to Marigot Bay for a day trip. Chris and Julie had become very friendly with Jim and Sheila, a Canadian couple. They were great fun and loved the sail. Marigot Bay is famous as the location for filming the Dr Doolittle film. It's rather up market and the Doolittle Restaurant over priced for what you get. I suppose like all famous sites they know there will always be customers wanting to visit and say I've been to Dr Doolittle's. We were no different. All said and done it was a nice to get out for a sail and visit somewhere different.

Just can't believe its Xmas day tomorrow. Joined the WCC Rally get together in The Rodney Bay Yacht Club for the World Rally boats which was due to depart for the San Blas islands on the 6th January. By strange coincidence one of the boats was owned by Graham who had previously looked after DwW for his friend Peter Dance so he knew everything about my boat. He wasn't exactly friendly - almost distant. I seem to get this impression quite a lot with fellow owners. Why are they so reticent to speak? Perhaps in this case he felt that it was below him to chat with a lowly ARC competitor. Perhaps I am being too critical and seeing into things too much. Joyce from FE joined us and collared the whole proceedings with a lecture on sails. I quietly left them to it. She means well. Left Marcus on his own but was concerned about leaving him alone.

Each time we walk to the Rodney Bay Beach area we pass a local guy called Edgar selling his carvings. I asked him if he carved in plastic as I was looking to replace the broken bracket for the autohelm. He managed to cobble something together but it didn't look too promising. Some days later

I returned to see all his carvings had disappeared. "You've had a good day" I said. "No man no good day they have been stolen". He hinted it may have been some tourist or visitor because the locals would not get away with it. He was very philosophical about it and confirmed the two carvings I had ordered would be ready in a couple of days. When I did collect them he also gave me a bracelet made from turtle. He insisted it was not killed but died naturally. Umh! I wondered if I was supporting this undesirable trade.

Father Christmas has lost his chimney

25th December. Is it really Xmas? Blue skies, warm air. We had organized a beach BBQ on a remote beach on the other side of the island named Cotton Beach. Here was a simple wooden restaurant named Marjorie's. On arrival we had to sign a petition to support her case to remain on the beach and not allow the existing hotel to take over the whole beach and extend its size.
I wish her well but somehow feel it's the old story of money talks.
The party spent the morning catamaran sailing whilst I did some windsurfing. Then we were served a large selection of Caribbean food on tables on the beach. It was so idyllic. Xmas in the Caribbean. WOW!
The music was very basic but who cares. The food and rum punches were in full flow.
Xmas Day on the beach, no washing up. A wish fulfilled. Diane and I both said we will revisit in the next few days on horseback and swim bareback.

Boxing Day was a heavy session indeed. It was the last day for Julie and Chris. I could see how much they were regretting having to return. For them it must have been a fantastic time. I will miss them both.

The Xmas day adventure must have had an impact because we returned to Cotton Bay or Cas en Bas beach by foot again. It was strange to walk along a remote path and see expensive villas and run down shacks as neighbours. Such a contrast. But I do wish the council could address the rubbish issue. Everywhere people just threw away their rubbish and it was an eyesore that could be solved with a little bit of care.

Do horses swim?

Again we returned to Cas en Bas beach for the third visit this one with the compliments of our son Jamie. It was his Xmas present to us and was a horse ride to go swimming on the horses. The forest ride was very sedate but when we reached the beach the horses were in their element. They swam out and allowed us to stand on their rumps.

Later that night met local bike hire chap who was trying to make a living out here. We learnt more about St Lucia in two hours than we had learnt in two weeks. In a nutshell there are the locals who look after each other and the non locals who have settled down from places such as the UK. These immigrants are never accepted even if they were born here and then moved to the UK. Then of course there are the tourists

Moved out of the hotel onto the boat. I know Diane is not entirely okay but costs are getting a bit out of hand I know she would prefer to stay in the hotel. Marcus is very quiet. I am not surprised; he must be missing his family terribly. He also revealed that Mary had cooled right off. I guess she has got cold feet which doesn't surprise me It's a big ask to take on Marcus's family baggage when she has a very settled life and well paid career.

31st December. Boat repair day. It seems strange that I should be working on the boat on New Years Eve. Raymarine sent the wrong belt for the drive wheel and the cost of sending 4 small strips of plastic for the spinnaker track from St Martin was £81.

That night we spent at The St Lucia Yacht Club. On the way there we stopped off at the bar Delirious Bay which is owned by Duncan a friend of Bill in the UK. He was glad to see us but completely immersed in preparing for the big night with a gigantic screen. Bill promised he would not fail to buy us a drink but with the stress of getting the show on the road he forgot. The whole of the Rodney Bay Town was absolutely packed and when we arrived at the YC the beach was swarming. An excellent BBQ and firework display all on the beach. No problems with rowdiness just everyone enjoying themselves. I'm sure people don't drink so much out here hence the peaceful and welcoming attitude of everyone. It's very refreshing to have youngsters coming up and saying hello.

New Year new adventures

As expected the first day of the year was very quiet. Even Gros Islet town was empty and was still dead when we returned that evening for their weekly Friday night party. The weekend is a public holiday here so apart from official celebrations everywhere was quiet.

We went on a tour with a taxi. They charge £90 for a day's tour of the island. Seems a lot of money but worth it for a good all round view of St Lucia. We passed processions and celebrations in Castries and Vieux Fort down the south of the island. This was quite a contrast between the tropical climate in the North and the much drier climate in the South. Lovely Botanical gardens in Soufriere. We passed a few bays on our tour but only a handful of boats in the bays. We saw Dennerys Town from the South promontory. A horse rider was galloping up and down the beach. The taxi driver had a relation in Vieux Fort so we did a quick detour to pick up his son who was staying there. He had a Man United shirt on and couldn't stop talking about the Premier Division. He knew all the teams and players. He even knew Crystal Palace.

Its now the first week in January and nearing the end of our stay in St Lucia. I fitted a Regulator for the Duogen to ensure that any surplus power generated is properly off loaded before burning out the electrics. Felt very relaxed as never before. Perhaps I am getting into the Caribbean lifestyle. It's nice just to relax on a quiet empty beach. This particular day I tried to stone a few crabs as they emerged from their little holes in the beach but they are much too quick. Further down the beach a young lad was playing in the water with his pony. Both were having great fun. The pony was highly excited and actually playing with the boy. Amazing sight.

The last day in Rodney bay was spent on the beach followed by a dinghy ride across the bay to a plush restaurant called The Edge. It's quite a little adventure to take your own dinghy to a restaurant. Beats getting the bus.

Next day I was beginning to worry about the next 6 months and returning to the UK. A faulty Solar Panel which undermined our total amps intake, a doubtful Auto helm which would be essential for our crossing and the laptop was showing a white vertical line on the screen. But what the hell I've come all this way so enjoy every minute. The problems will get sorted one way or another.

The World Arc boats leave today. Wish I had as big a boat as the competitors. The minimum qualifying length is 40 feet. The ARC is only 27 feet. Does this have a meaning?

Off to the airport

The plan is to sail down to Vieux Fort, drop Diane at the airport and at the same time pick up Graham who will join us for the next 6 months. Diane was not seasick and our first stop should have been Anse la Raye which has superb fish restaurants. We sailed straight past it and onto Anse Cochon. Lovely bay and beach however Diane was not happy with the sailing and that was upsetting me as well.

The next day Marcus went off snorkeling in the dinghy and returned with some nasty sting rashes on his arm. Possibly a jellyfish. Diane not happy and anchor is dragging so we return to Anse la Raye which didn't look at all inviting so decided to go back to Rodney bay with a stop over in Marigot Bay. Very frustrating as I was keen to see The Pitons in Soufriere. Once again we found anchoring not holding in Marigot Bay so paid for a mooring buoy. I can only presume that the sand around these parts is very hard and the anchor is not sinking in the sand. The strong winds around at the moment persuaded us to err on the side of caution and tie up to a buoy.

Bats in the Belfry

That night we had a nice reasonably priced dinner in Marigot Marina. I was surprised after seeing all the posh boats around. Then we had a drink in The Marigot Hotel where it will set you back £300 per night. Very plush. Just Diane's 'cup of tea'. Wish I had drunk a few more beers because it was a long night. Hot, stuffy, mosquitoes and would you believe it Bats. I was sleeping in the main saloon because of the heat and at sometime in the night I was awoken by a sort of fluttering noise. It kept on so I opened my eyes and saw a black object flash by, then another and another with some of them stopping below the ceiling netting and sucking on the bananas. Next morning the bunk under the netting was smothered in half digested banana. What a mess.

Back to Rodney Bay which seemed almost like returning home. Managed to buy some frozen Dorado fish which we ate on the boat. Washed down with a cold beer to start with wine and whisky to finish. Must watch my intake of booze. A fitting end to Diane's trip.

Tomorrow she returns to the UK and I have my regular bout of poor confidence and doubt. Stop it. You are living in Paradise.

We were moored up alongside Roger who had kindly loaned us an electric plug converter. He was planning to have his boat permanently moored in the Caribbean and fly out for regular breaks. He spoke of the advantages of having a boat permanently here but I wasn't convinced regarding travel costs and time from home to make it viable.

His boat was tailor-made for his comforts, air conditioning throughout and two large fridges from which he gave us a couple of ice cold beers. I also tried his recommended Martinique Rum but it was far too sweet for me. Marcus kept taking beer after beer without a mention of buying or getting repleshments from our boat. I was quite embarrassed. Not Marcus, he had no scruples where freebies were concerned. The word Sponger came to mind.

Off to Airport again

This time it's just Marcus and I and our first stop was Soufriere and The Pitons. What a setting in a beautiful sunset. So wish Diane liked sailing. Had a very pleasant snorkel in Bat Cove with lots of pretty fish.

Diane texted to say her plane had been diverted to Glasgow. The captain was not happy with the CAA at Gatwick as he didn't think the diversion was necessary for a small flurry of snow. It took Diane another 12 hours extra after coaching back down to Gatwick through some rather rough snow conditions. If only they knew what the rest of the winter would bring.

Next stop Labourie . Arrived after strong head wind and opted for a mooring due to fresh winds. The town was so much nicer than the busier towns of Soufriere and Castries.Whilst the beach was unspoilt with Palm Trees lapping the waters edge. We had a very large item to tick off our list. It was live lobster and this place was recommended. We were soon looked after by a local woman who couldn't do enough to help. "Come with me "she beckoned and a few minutes walk along the beach we met her brother. A rather large young unfit lad who looked as if he sat on his little beach chair for most of the day.

I wonder if the people of the Caribbean adapted this laissez faire attitude before they come here or it was part of their makeup. It's something I wondered because15 years before when I had visited St Martin the Island was very industrious, well developed and very efficient. That Island is administered by the Dutch and the French, whereas St Lucia is what I would call 'indigenous'. I wonder if I will visit an island that combines the best of both such as Caribbean friendliness, helpfulness and chilled out ambience with European efficiency, cleanliness and industriousness.

That aside we were introduced to the local fisherman who pointed to a submerged cage 30 metres off shore. He waded out to his boat and I joined him to fetch the lobsters from the cage. I chose two medium sized specimens and noticed that they had no claws. They were Crayfish. I asked for a bag to carry them back to the boat but strange as it may sound plastic bags are either not readily available or they are a very useful item so people hold onto them. Anyway our young guide managed to find a cardboard box and off we went to cook our supper. It took a bit of organizing but managed to cook each one before they scrambled out of the pot. This was Marcus's first real taste of lobster. He was not disappointed. Lots of meat in the tail rather than the claws.

Sailed to Vieux Fort the next day and managed to moor alongside quay in harbour with the help of the locals. They wanted paying just for securing the mooring lines from the stern to the quayside. I gave a couple of pounds to one of the older guys who seemed the only one who knew what he was doing. Of course the others were up in arms. Almost like throwing a piece of meat to a load of wild dogs. The need to get clearance off St Lucia was my first experience of Caribbean customs and excise (the procedure in Rodney bay was smoothed over by the WCC people). The problem is that the officers have a set routine for air travellers but not for yachts so I spent a good hour betwixt and between immigration and customs. It seems they rarely speak with one another. What a mess. I hope it gets better.

The airport appears to be very close to the marina on the map. Not so. I arranged for a taxi to take me to pick up Graham with an hour's stop off at the windsurfing beach. Wow, I could spend some time here. Lovely beach, perfect wind direction and no boats in the way. Unfortunately again we were limited for time but I did sit in the beach bar for half an hour waiting for the taxi to return. Then I spotted Roger our neighbour in Rodney bay. He was killing an hour before catching his flight home. He was most put out that I preferred an orange drink to a beer. I get the impression he likes his tipple.

This was later confirmed by Graham who told of a skipper whom he helped bring his boat over to Antigua a couple of months ago. The skipper had two fridges piled high with cool beers. It was none other than Roger on his boat Vittoria. It's a small world.

Went on to the airport and after a two hour delay met Graham and took him back to the boat. Bought a nice fresh Tuna in the harbour. Our plan was to move the boat and anchor outside the harbour have dinner then set off to Bequia about 21.00 hours. The Tuna was delicious.

Sixth Step to Heaven - Touring the Caribbean

15th Jan 2010 -

Following the coast down the windward side of St Vincent proved a little bit of a challenge as it was now dark and I was taking watch with Graham. A sudden gust of wind caught us by surprise and I had difficulty getting the twin headsail in. Marcus came up and with the two of us we soon had the boat steadied. I don't think Graham was too impressed after spending 8 hours on a flight and then thrown in at the deep end. On reflection we should have rested in Vieux Fort and left by early light.

We arrived in Bequia about 6.30 am and after many attempts managed to get the anchor set. I'm sure we are being too fussy about getting the entire anchor head buried. But to be fair we were experiencing quite fresh winds and it was quite busy with lots of boats moored very close.

The customs procedure went quite well possibly because this was a favourite bay for starting and finishing touring The Grenadines. More importantly the customs officers and the immigration officers shared the same building and seemed to talk with each other. The town was typical West Indian Caribbean with open drainage, rubbish and shanty town houses but nice friendly helpful people.

It was a Sunday and all the locals were going to church. Everyone sang gospels and the children looked so smart especially the little girls with their white cotton shirts, bright colored socks and pigmy tail hair styles.

There was a good breeze around so I got Marcus and Graham to tow me with the windsurfing gear over to the beach and as usual the wind dropped and was too slight for a sail. Also there were a lot of boats coming in to anchor off. So I spent a good two hours on the beach with no sun cream waiting for the dinghy to return. They turned up paddling the boat as the engine had packed up again. This time I was told it looked serious with blue smoke coming out of the engine. Not a good day.

Cannot say I was too impressed with Bequia. It was supposed to be a recommended place to visit. Our next stop was a short brisk bumpy trip to Mustique. Compulsory buoy mooring off beach and small ferry jetty. Very quick and friendly immigration and customs registration. A beautiful Island with empty beaches and well managed walks through the forests and salt marshes. Paths well signed with information and the town was clean and tidy. One sign had two tortoises humping and a quote underneath from the John Lennon song Beautiful Boy "life is what happens to you while you're busy making other plans"

This island was populated with some very rich people owning very lavish villas, Mick Jagger, Lord Snowden. I think one would need a certain reputation and loads of money to get a place here.

We visited the gorgeous beaches and then toured the town to buy some fresh fish. There was the inevitable working population quarters which looked very smart indeed. The local fishermen had their own little huts, presumably supplied compliments of the islands administrators and there was a lobster cage full of very large crayfish ready for the restaurants and local dignitaries. Next to the fish market was this large pile of empty conches. I took one as a memento. The outside was coated with barnacles and crustaceans but inside it had a beautiful iridescent pink shell. They are apparently quite expensive in the UK. Here they were just rubbish.

Later that day we got chatting with the boat moored close by. It was occupied by 5 very raucous Boston women and a skipper who did all the boat bits. They were all old school friends here for a good time without their partners and letting their hair down. We joined them for a laugh and a swim. They were great fun and cheered me up no end.

We spent that evening in the famous Basils Blues bar, as usual great music but expensive food and empty and no atmosphere. I had a chicken and prawn stew but no gravy. No gravy in a stew?? Sent it back. The bill was 200 euros for us three. God knows how much it would have cost in the more expensive Cotton House Restaurant up the hill.

All said and done Mustique is worth every penny. A superb Island.

The Grenadines

We decided that the best port of call for doing repairs to the boat would be Union Island so we set off to sail there before visiting Tobago Cays.

They had a very good marina for such a small and remote Island. It even had electricity on the pontoon! It also had a good Yacht Club with a couple of restaurants and a fish pool with real live sharks swimming around. I felt a bit sorry for them as it was only a small pool. Also on display a few pictures which were excellent drawings of the area but at 800 euros. I suppose they wanted to add a bit of culture and sophistication to their Club. In the morning I visited the local outboard engine specialist. He didn't speak much English but I could understand enough to get the jist. The engine needed a new impeller which he couldn't source. So another session on the phone to Diane to get a Seagull Sports impeller shipped out. Diane didn't have much luck but I managed to trace a supplier in Brighton of all places. I was beginning to cotton on to the high cost of making phone calls from my mobile. But it had to be done. On the way back I saw a rough wood sign for The Anchorage YC. It had OPEN and CLOSE on it but the OPEN letters were upside down. I thought this sums up the Caribbean for me. I chuckled inside.

I had eventually managed to get the right drive belt from Raymarine and fitted this.

Later I saw a lone windsurfer going like the clappers across the Bay. I finished off my work and with the help of Marcus took my board and kit around the bay to a little inlet where I could launch. Success at last. I managed to get planeing and steer through the anchored boats without too much messing around.

We spent that evening in the Anchorage YC. Marcus didn't want to eat so I said to Graham let us eat. He declined my offer and said he wanted Marcus to eat with us. But Marcus didn't want to eat with us. So Graham got all sulky. I was personally rather put out that he didn't want to eat on his own with me. How odd?

The next day I went back to the little bay it was literally a 150 yard walk and it was deserted with three empty villas. A local told me later this area used to be very select and then a hurricane destroyed the concrete pontoon and the villas. This is a common story in the Caribbean. But he also said there is good snorkeling under the broken pontoon. He was right. This was my first glimpse of coral fish. They were beautiful.

We spent our last night in Clifton Town. Very Caribbean except for a lively Bar and restaurant full of French Canadians all living on Union Island. We left Marcus supping beers. I think he wanted to get a few down him.

Heaven or Paradise? Palm Island, the Grenadines

January 22nd. Sailed to Palm Island just a few miles away from Union Island. Superb beach and typical Caribbean setting with no one in sight. We had to get to Salt Whistle Bay so didn't actually stop. When we arrived we dropped the anchor 5 times to try and get it fixed but ended up with it lying on its side with 6 x length of chain. It held all night despite a fresh breeze. In the morning we admired the pelicans diving for fish. They are so adept. Also our first sight of Frigate birds. This is a lovely protected Bay.

Onto Tobago Cays which was easy enough to navigate. We arrived by 9am so spent the whole day snorkeling and swimming with the turtles. They are not afraid and don't mind people diving alongside them. They spend all their time grazing on the seaweed. Almost like Cows in a field. There's only a small beach here but the surrounding reefs are fantastic with special buoys to tie up the dinghy. The coral and fish were spectacular.

The different and vivid colour blues that coincided with the various depths will remain in mind forever. Also found Iguanas on the beach and stingrays swimming around the boat.

This area has to be seen to be believed. True Paradise.

After two days we had to depart for our return to Bequia. I could have stayed here for ever in paradise.

On our way to Bequia Graham tried his hand at fishing and put out a hand line. I also decided to have a go despite Gr showing chamoncern about having two lines off the back. The inevitable happened and we spent an age trying to untangle the mess. I ended up cutting my line and leaving Graham to sort out his line. I guess this was the start of our deteriorating relationship.

We anchored in Bequia Bay and sorted out bits and pieces for the boat. So many jobs. Half shroud was damaged, GPS playing up, Outboard engine requires new impeller, PC laptop has a defunct screen and new rowlocks for dinghy have snapped after 10 days use.

Spent time on the mobile ordering new impeller and new outboard engine to be collected in Dominica. Asked Diane to buy a new laptop. Should be able to get new GPS Antennae in next port of call on Martinique.

Passage Plan or no passage plan

The passage to Martinique was 90 miles and Graham was insistent on formulating a passage plan with estimated times, tides, winds etc, etc. I told him in no uncertain terms that I do not do textbook sailing especially when we don't know what the wind direction will do during the 90 miles. Similar to Marcus I prefer to set sail to see where the wind is before planning our passage. He was not happy and kept quoting textbook stuff with plan A and Plan B etc, etc

As it turned out the wind was directly on our forward bow side and pushing us away from the leeward side of St Vincent and St Lucia. The wind and cloud gathered and soon we were being pushed far too west to get to Martinique directly. The wind starting increasing and never dipping below 30 knots with gusts of 45 knots. It was soon apparent we were way off Martinique and after much argument decided to cut our journey short and turn right to Rodney Bay rather than spend half the night tracking up and across to Marin marina. It was the right decision. Graham was not happy with our passage making. He thought we should have been tacking all the way up rather than getting so far west. Possibly he was right but it was the beginning of a very strained relationship. He had great difficulty communicating and this affected his ability to manage stressful situations.

I was not happy with the unscheduled stop in St Lucia. I had too many fond memories with Diane. No sooner had we departed for Martinique when Graham started again on his navigation argument. We should be tacking across to get to Marin Marina he persisted. Marcus and I thought we may as well go with the wind for now and hope that it changes for the better and the current, what little there is may help us later on.

So by the time we were in striking distance of Martinique we were once again too far west and had to motor across the bottom of the Island to reach Marin marina. Perhaps Graham was right about tacking up and across but he just didn't have the ability to discuss matters in a friendly way. I wouldn't like to be a crew member under his skippering. It would be so unfriendly and negative.

The French Disconnection

This wind is not going away. Not a very nice final few hours against a headwind gusting 45 knots. By the time we arrived we were one day late due to our stop over in Rodney Bay. In typical French tradition we were kept waiting for a pontoon mooring.

With so many repairs to complete we planned to stay on Martinique for 4 days.

The French inhabitants were very well organized and the island has good roads, communications and croissants of course. The marina is also very well represented. The rigger was very good and as soon as I took the damaged half shroud in for repair he replaced it the next day.

Diane had also done a great job sending me a new impeller so I took the outboard engine to be fixed by a French mechanic highly recommended in the pilot book. What I didn't expect was his comprehensive hatred of my outboard engine. He explained that it was a Selva and they had bought the Seagull brand presumably to try and improve their image. He was adamant that he was not going to work on the engine. I couldn't believe my bad luck. After much begging he did agree just to replace the impeller. When I went back the next day all hopeful and happy he told me the engine would not start and his hatred had been exemplified. This was not a good day. He didn't have another engine he could sell but offered a new one for 1500 Euros. No thank you. I got on the blower later that day and ordered a new Mercury 2.5 hp engine from a supplier in Dominica for 500 euros.

That wasn't the end. The next day was a Saturday and the electronics guy only worked in the morning. So more pleading and begging for help. I wish I spoke French. It would be very useful out here. To be fair they were very helpful and after a few frustrating hours managed to replace the old antennae and get the GPS working. I wasn't looking forward to the bill. This is not a cheap island and my budget had already been blown out of the water. To top it all my Santander card was declined and my Barclaycard expired. When it rains it pours.

With all the organizing I didn't spend a lot of time getting to see the town and surrounding countryside but did get to see the old traditional wooden boat racing. They had some 6 or so old boats that had one enormous sail shaped like a Chinese junk. They also rowed the boat to go faster. It was a good show with lots of people celebrating and singing.

Marcus spent all his time on his laptop. Ever since leaving St Lucia he had signed up with lots of on-line dating companies and was now well and truly into laptop speak. He had at least three dates lined up for when he returned to the UK. He was obsessed with the interaction. This was not the women hater that I knew from back in the UK. Perhaps he had finally shaken off his past bad experiences of women.

This particular evening he returned from his laptop lovemaking session in the bar and started to play Stairway to Heaven by Rolf Harris - which is an insult to the greatest original track by Led Zeppelin - just to wind me up. Marcus had this sad schoolboy playground mentality. This was not the time for jokes and I exploded. I told him never to play that song again. He knew I was serious.

Our stay in Martinique was not the best and I was glad to be on our way to Dominique as soon as I had settled the bill for the Garmin GPS Antennae - 400 Euros. It did not shock me. By now I was like a condemned man who had accepted his fate. Astronomical costs would not stop me enjoying myself. I was determined to enjoy paradise. On the bright side it was nice to get the boat back to shipshape condition.

One cannot help but notice Diamond Rock which lies just off Martinique and has quite a reputation. In the days of when Bonaparte was at his height of success there was this impudent Englishman called Nelson who couldn't take Martinique as a strategic point for controlling the area. So as funds were not available to dispatch a warship specifically to guard this part he decided to occupy Diamond Rock with cannon and supplies. Bonaparte was not amused and sent Villeneuve to get rid of the damned English. He sort of succeeded but not to Bonaparte's satisfaction and so Villeneuve became out of favour. Of course history will tell that the two great admirals met again at Trafalgar. Villeneuve survived despite losing the battle. As we passed between the rock and the mainland I thought of the sailors that managed to hoist all their equipment and firearms and live on this small rock.

We stopped off at St Pierre which used to be the capital of Martinique before disaster struck. A volcano exploded and killed all 30,000 inhabitants of the town except for one who was being held prisoner on a charge of murder deep in a cell. Life is a funny thing sometimes. Then we passed IIe deTrois where Josephine was born.

The Eco Island

Dominica – 3rd Feb

Picked up new Mercury outboard engine and now I could relax knowing the boat was fully equipped except for the faulty Solar panel. Graham had visited this island before and wanted to complete his wish to see Desolation Valley which is in the middle of the island and an 8 hour return trip. On our way up to where we began our trek we were held up for an hour traversing through some major roadworks. The driver told us the president of Equador had donated 20 million for its construction. Equador must be a very rich third world country. I suppose it must be something to do with oil reserves. The distance to the middle isn't that far but the trek is through tropical forests and very hilly in places. The valley is made up of very pungent Sulphuric springs. We plastered ourselves with the hot mud which should be kept on for a few hours to benefit from its medicinal powers. Further on are the famous Boiling Lakes. Again lots of hot sulphur with a temperature of 145 degrees centigrade in the middle of the lake. I was careful not to fall in. We stopped for a very pleasant 40 degree sulphur bath. It was hard to get out as it was so relaxing. When we returned back to base I swam under a waterfall in a hidden gorge. The water was chilled but not unbearable.

For once Graham was happy and quite enjoyed the evening when we met up with 3 young Dominican girls. They were so friendly and quite sophisticated with their own cars and apartments. This was in contrast to the Island which was more of the Caribbean style and poorer than say Martinique but so much more welcoming and friendly. One of the girls invited us around to her place and gave us cool beers. She had no other agenda just open welcoming hospitality. So refreshing. We met them later in a cheap and cheerful fish restaurant. Like an idiot I drank their local Rum. Beware of local brews in the Caribbean they are not hangover friendly.

Four whinges and you're out

No 1. Whilst in town I bought another Digicel simcard following another run in with Virgin, who had cut me off with no prior warning for exceeding my credit allowance.

No 2. I also bought a carton of milk because Graham had decided that I should have black coffee like him and Marcus and therefore had thrown out the last carton of milk and the instant powdered milk. What a strange person. I could have taken umbrance to such stupid action. But I just let it go.

No 3. It was past Diane's birthday but I wanted to send some flowers. Not an easy operation with my laptop out of commission and the local internet café showing American flower web sites including Interflora USA. I just couldn't get them to recognize the address where she was staying with her father in Norwich. So frustrating.

No 4. Phoned Barden yet again for a resolution to the solar panel but they are now in dispute with Solara the German manufacturer who will not accept responsibility. I wish I had never dealt with these incompetent people.

Rousseau, the capital of Dominica, was interesting with old colonial type houses very similar to Florida Keys. I was very impressed with the Islands stance on Eco preservation. They did not have the number of lovely beaches and holiday type places such as St Lucia so they were promoting their natural resources such as tropical forests, indigenous birds and animals and natural living. One part of this was a place called Champagne Bay. Here you could swim off the rocks amongst the coral fish and loads of bubbles escaping from the seabed. Quite an experience.

Pirates of the Caribbean

On the way up the coast we decided to stop off in Portsmouth which has a famous bar called Big Papas. Lots of the usual photos of yesterday's celebrities but not a lot of action.

We booked a water taxi trip up the river which was the scene for the second Pirates of the Caribbean film. Very eerie and quiet. The oarsman gave us his usual spiel about a mangrove tree that once had a giant boa constrictor sitting on it. Then I asked him why there were no parrots around. Especially as the bird was their national patron?? He replied that they are very shy and only appear in the early morning or evening. I was convinced that all the parrots have either been shot or hunted to extinction in the Caribbean. Graham said I should visit Richmond Park when I return home where there are plenty of wild parrots.

He appeared to be completely disinterested with new discoveries or new places. Very sad.

Back with the Frenchies

On the way to Guadaloupe are the Illes de Saints: a set of beautiful islands with lovely beaches and the influence of French colonization. It was just like arriving in Brittany but with 30 degrees and sandy beaches. The town was so French chic. Similar to Martinique but much more relaxed and friendly. Bought another Sarong to replace my worn and torn original. Took the dinghy over to the other island with my windsurfing gear. Not a bad session as I managed to borrow a bigger board from one of the French locals. He owned the local diving and water sports shop and explained how he closes every afternoon and goes windsurfing/ kite surfing with his mates who are also shopkeepers. Not a bad life I thought. Lost my flip-flops. Like an idiot I left them on the sugar scoop when we went out for the evening. Of course I never thought that the boat moves around in the water. They were floating around the Bay somewhere. Sometimes I wonder where my brain is.

The Butterfly Gap

Guadaloupe has a shape very similar to a butterfly. To get to the north one can either go around the outside or navigate through the middle via a small river. It's times like this that I do plan a passage very carefully so I was very well prepared for what was needed.

The South approach has a bridge which opens once a day at 5.00am. Before the channel approach there is a very wide Bay that does not mark the passage very well. To be fair with Graham he had programmed his handheld GPS so when we temporarily lost our way he guided us through to the channel approach. His thoughts about our lack of passage making plans were fully vindicated in his mind and I could see he was very highly stressed during this little episode. Marcus and I were not fazed, we knew we would eventually find our way to the channel marker buoy and there was plenty of water under our hull. We were not impressed with his 'holier than thou' attitude.

We anchored off the entrance to the Bridge and went through the next morning in pitch darkness. The channel was marked but it had lots of bends and shallow parts if you strayed off line. But by 08.30 we had navigated the river and were moored up in the small harbour of Port Louis on the North east coast of Guadaloupe.

After such a successful trip to get there it was very disappointing to discover that the Immigration and customs office was closed. I tried to find out from both the post office and the police station when we might be able to get our papers stamped but with little success. After two hours waiting outside the office I came to the conclusion the officer was not about to appear for the day. Reluctantly I returned to the boat and told Marcus and Graham we would have to go back around the outside of the Island to a busier town called Deshaies. We thought about carrying on to Antigua without clearance from Guadalupe. But with the experiences we already had I wasn't going to argue the toss with such officious organizations. I didn't fancy us spending a night in a customs jail. How frustrating. It took us a good part of 4 hours to motor over to Deshais. By which time it was getting late so we anchored off and went into town to clear papers. Again another session of getting the Immigration officer to stamp our papers.

This whole business is just so frustrating; time consuming, annoying and unnecessary.

An incredible sunset

As the evening approached I noticed that the sky had become extremely dark. I thought we were in for a terrific downpour and everyone was looking West over towards the direction of Montserrat. The sunset was unbelievable. There was a gap between the dark blue sky and the horizon which set off the brightness of the sun. Then it happened. It started to rain down with Ash. The volcano had erupted. By the morning the boat was covered in 3 inches of Ash. It took us hours to wash down the decks but the ash was so fine it seeped into every nook and cranny. I was concerned with the damage it might cause to the electronics. There was nothing we could do except keep our fingers crossed.

A very very sad day

February 11th. Today I received a call nobody ever wants to receive. My stepfather had passed away. A few days earlier Diane had described John's condition as very poorly and he was in intensive care with blood poisoning (septicaemia?) but somehow I never thought it was serious and knew he would pull through. Since my Mum died 5 years ago John had never been the same. She was the light of his life which had previously been rather sad with a long unhappy marriage. He had spent 35 years of married bliss with Mum and although Mum was widowed she completely changed from a traditional old fashioned stay at home mother and wife to liberated single woman with a life of her own. They were perfectly matched. My father died when I was 26 years old so I knew John my stepfather longer. He was a lovely fellow and I miss him lots.

My brother rang the next day. I have never known him to be so upset.

We were on the way to Antigua when I received the call from Diane. She was insistent that I should stay out here and not return for the funeral. Especially as our son Matthew was on his way here with his friend Miles. I was in a different mind and planned to return to the UK. I gave myself a week to decide.

We moored up in Falmouth Harbour. Our boat was like a small dinghy alongside the enormous gin palaces with their smart uniformed crew and red carpet on the pontoon.

There was a water shortage on the Island so we couldn't get water to hose the boat down. There were still lots of Ash remaining but we managed to make do with sea water.

It was rather amusing to see all the big boats getting their daily wash despite the water shortage. They must have enormous tanks on board.

I bet they used all the water from the pontoon before we arrived. That's why there's a shortage on the Island.

When it rains it pours

Further distressing news from the UK. My youngest sister in law has been diagnosed with lymphatic cancer. She is only 55. They told her mistakenly on Xmas Eve she had a few months to live. What a thing to handle at such a time of year. Then a few days later they admitted it was not necessarily terminal and with chemo she had a better chance of survival.

My other sister in law rang Diane saying her mother was on her last legs. The worse thing for me was not having my family around to share my grief. It was a low point in my life.

Marcus in his usual discreet way wanted to go out and celebrate the completion of his 'Six steps' since he was due to return to the UK shortly. I had a very quiet night on the boat.

13th Feb. Took a walk over to English Harbour which is literally 10 minutes away. It's a much nicer marina and we should have parked up here. It had a great atmosphere being Nelsons Dockyard. Many of the buildings were restored and the history was all around. Easy to imagine 200 years ago with the old warships anchored up and hundreds of sailors and workmen milling around. It was a pleasant break from the boat but the next morning I awoke feeling very low. John's death, family illnesses, continuing boat concerns about Step 7 and sailing back to the UK. I felt like walking away from it all. A few tears welled up. Can I endure? Diane's suggestion of shipping the boat back was beginning to sound attractive.

Not for long. There was no way I could face myself. My pride would be severely dented and how could I face life. No, no, no.

Sunday 14th Feb Spent the evening with Marcus on Shirley Heights. Magnificent view over English Harbour and the bay. The sunset was stunning and they put on a musical show each Sunday. The entertainment was top quality and Marcus was really getting in the groove. I had no heart for it.

Sailed round to Jolly Harbour. What a beautiful approach with iridescent green and turquoise waters but very milky. I thought it might have been the Volcano effect but it seems it is always like this. I took to the marina instantly. Very well laid out and with excellent facilities including an international standard boat yard for hurricane shelter and hot showers – the first since Rodney Bay. I think originally this Marina was going to be another large International Yacht Harbour. There is a ginormous supermarket just 100 yards away and it's a short walk to one of the best beaches iv'e seen so close to the Marina. And the customs and immigration was all in one office and friendly.

The funeral was set for the 26th Feb and Barbara had managed to track down a reasonable air fare for me to return to the UK. I had promised myself I would return if I could get a ticket for less than £1000. It was £900.

Matthew and his friend were due the next day and Graham wanted to sail off to Barbuda returning in a few days for my return to the UK. I explained that it was not fair to expect two non sailors to set off on a long trip on a difficult passage. He was not happy and quoted my crew wanted advert stating a fully crewed boat offering open passages around the Caribbean. He cannot expect me to deliver paradise all the time – I told him so in no uncertain way.

More boat bits

Replacement Solar panel held up in Antigua customs. I told Barden quite clearly not to deliver to me by person and send it addressed to the boat. This apparently avoids tax and customs restrictions. So I had to hire a freight agent to pick it up from the airport at a cost of £90. The alternative was for me to spend all day walking around the various airport offices getting the right papers signed off. No thanks.

Finally managed to track down replacement bracket for the Auto pilot so ordered two from Raymarine.

Time for change

This was Marcus's last day before returning to the UK. I noticed he had packed all of his belongings which I questioned as he would be returning to the boat for Step 7. "I might want to sail in the UK" he said. In the middle of winter I thought? This is a bit odd but he assured me that as long as he got work he would be back. I emphasized how important it was for him to return.

We had a few drinks that evening and discussed crewing requirements for the rest of the trip. I said I was fed up with Graham's whinging and sulking and considering asking him to leave the boat. Marcus nodded and said I was quite capable of getting around with a novice crew but questioned the shortage of crew for Step 7.

Little did I know that Graham had his own secret plans?

17th Feb. Spent all day at the airport waiting for Matthew. Eventually they announced the flight had been diverted to Guadeloupe with technical problems. They turned up later that evening knackered but very excited. Of course I was concerned about Graham being happy with two non sailors but after a couple of beers he warmed to them. Perhaps because he had no axe to grind with them yet.

Matthew loved the Beach in Jolly Harbour and Miles a fanatical fisherman was overcome by the big 5 foot Tarpins jumping around in the Marina when the fishing boats came back and threw the remains of their catch off the quayside. Tarpins are world renowned as excellent game fish but not good for eating. Miles had already managed to catch one together with a few good sized Snappers.

Matthew had brought the new Laptop out with him. It was fine but took some setting up with Mailasail and the likes because it was a 64 bit operating system. It was good of him to load all the software. Not a simple job.

Terry sent a text message asking if I would do the speech for John's funeral. I suppose as the eldest member of the family it's my duty.

18th Feb. Set off for the Islands off North Antigua. Lots of reefs around and navigation important but should be Ok as long as we take care. The first stop was to anchor off Jumby Bay which is across the waters from the mainland and the airport. They ferry holiday makers in directly from the airport and it's very exclusive.

As soon as we arrive on the beach in the dinghy two burly security guys came up and said gruffly we can stay on the beach but not any further. This did not impress. They can stuff their hotel which costs £2500 per night to stay.

Miles had walked over to a small reef to sus out the fishing. He returned all excited after spotting a couple of Bone Fish which he was keen to catch. So off he went with rod in hand. He didn't have any luck but that night both he and Matthew caught more Snapper fish. We had fresh fish to last us days.

We carried on down to Great Bird Island. There are no channel markers so it's all eyeball navigation. The sun was out so we could spot the reefs and thread our way through. There were just a few boats scattered around the big island and other smaller ones. Very quiet and peaceful with good anchorage and some reasonable snorkeling. As soon as we drop anchor Miles and Matthew are off in the dinghy with their rods. They just love it all.

Was so pleased with Matthew. He was very polite and helpful and happy to share domestics with everyone. He did have an issue with having to helm but I explained as captain and not as a son to father relationship that he must be seen to be pulling his weight.

He was ok after that and took his duty on the helm when required.

Our time together is so good. I was so pleased we were getting on. Good to see him eating healthily after his food poisoning episode back home.

Big time fishing

Miles and Matthew really getting into fishing. Miles caught a very large sting ray but cut the line before bringing it on board. We didn't want to be messing around with a 40 lb ray with a very long tail. Then to top it all Miles catches his dream fish. A 15lb Red Snapper. I cut it up into 10 large steaks. They had learnt to put a very light line on the last metre before the hook so the snapper fish could not detect the trap. They also had a very small hook. Squid proved the most successful bait. As soon as the evening came they both would be at it until very late. On our final morning here

Matthew wanted to see the sun rise so we both got up at 5 am and took the dinghy over to the Island peak to see the sun come up. I was more impressed with Matthew's drive and determination to do something he wanted to do so enthusiastically.

The boat is beginning to stink of old bait now we have been out for some days. On the way back to Jolly Harbour we made two stops. The first was Dickenson Bay with good anchorage and plenty of room. Very popular beach mostly taken up by a huge Sandals Hotel complex. We then stopped off in Deep Bay for a swim and snorkel. The wreck in the middle promised some good snorkeling but it was too deep to reach without diving gear so we had our Snapper lunch and headed back. Nice to return to a hot shower and ice cold beer in Jolly Harbour. And would you believe it? – no repairs needed to DwW

24th Feb UK Bound.

Off to airport full of trepidation for the coming week. Arrived in Gatwick after 7 hour journey. It was wet, windy and cold. Took a lot of adjusting to family, friends and finding things in the house. The time lag was giving me problems. Very restless at night.

The funeral went well with dozens of Johns bowling friends attending. My speech was just a story about John's life with Mum and the family. It was straight from the heart. Everyone complimented on the words.

Tina looked absolutely drained and so pale. The chemo must be hard to take. I'm amazed that she attended. Why is it that bad luck seems to always affect the best people? No justice in this world.

1st March-I return to paradise

Picked up Barbara from Lancing and arrived in Antigua after a delayed flight of 9 hours. So good to have the sun on my back. Spent the day on the beach unwinding and planning our trip to Barbuda. That evening it was Rum punches all round with Barbara having one too many so I helped her back to the boat. It was good to see her relaxed and happy after her recent upsets. Matthew showed me a picture of their Fishing Trip on a charter boat; it was a Wahoo at least 5 foot long and weighing 20 lbs. It was good to be back.

Set off for Barbuda and stopped in Dickenson Bay again to give us a good daytime sail to our destination. Had an easy passage to Barbuda except for Larry the auto helm playing up. Here we go again thinking negative thoughts about having a reliable autopilot for the UK return. The Island approach is relatively simple. The secret is to stay well west of the reef that extends some 15 miles south east of the Island. There are 300 wrecks on this reef. Most accidents occurred many years ago when there was no GPS and boats coming from the East Atlantic and Europe cut across the reef thinking they were well clear of any trouble.

There was a brisk wind and a big swell but we anchored OK. Certainly too rough for landing our dinghy which has a soft bottom. We watched another dinghy returning to their boat and despite having a good sized engine and hard bottom they still had to get the crew to swim out over the shore break. But what a fabulous beach. Unbelievable site.

The following day was slightly better so we decided it was worth the risk to launch the dinghy. I was not very happy after my two previous experiences and worried for Barbara if we capsized. "None of it" she cried. I was most impressed with her bravery and "anything you can do I can do also" attitude. We did manage to beach but very nearly capsized. I must remember next time not to throttle down too soon. To avoid the shore break effect the engine should be kept at full revs right up to the beach.

It was true what they said in the brochures. The Beach was like walking on a lovely soft springy bed and had a distinctly pinky colour. We walked over the ridge to the Lagoon side which was literally 30 yards and got a water taxi to the Capital Codrington. It's a very English type town and when I eventually found the Immigration office the lady was very helpful. "Thomas surname eh? Most of the islands inhabitants are Thomas here" she said. I did note that all the admin work on these small islands were completed by the women. I wondered what the men did.
It didn't take long to explore the Capital it was no bigger than a small English village. We took the ferry up to the north of the lagoon to tour the

Frigate Bird sanctuary. This is the largest one in the world. The birds were used to boats turning up so we could almost touch them. Just a few yards away was another little inlet with a dilapidated bird watching pontoon. "Why is it not used" I asked. "The birds got fed up with all the tourists and moved their nests up here 100 yards away" he replied.

Getting back to the boat was not going to be easy. We discussed the best tactics with the now familiar moaning from Graham because it was so stressful for him. The first attempt failed with Barbara stuck in the dinghy still shore bound so we decided that Matthew and I would launch the dinghy and Graham would swim back. Success. I dropped Matthew off and returned for Barbara. I got as close to the beach as possible without capsizing the dinghy but it was still a struggle for Barbara getting through the shore break but she kept going and then tried to get into the dinghy but the sides were too high. She managed to swim about three quarters of the way back but was definitely tiring. She hung on to the side whilst I gently throttled up. The force of the dinghies forward motion swept Barbara's legs underneath and the propeller caught her foot. Luckily it was only a graze. The whole trip today should not have been taken. Much too risky.

But we would never have been happy not seeing Barbuda Beach and walking along its pink sand. This will be a lasting picture in my mind.

As for Graham we had granted his wish to visit Barbuda and all he could say was the bird sanctuary and island tour was a bit boring. He reminds me of the sulky boy called Kevin in the Harry Enfield show. How can a mature adult be so childish?

The best snorkeling in Barbuda was located a good half mile off the beach and we could see the overfalls, but with the wind that we were experiencing it would have been another daunting escapade. Oh well another time perhaps.

We spent the next morning relaxing whilst we waited for a favourable departure time and a kind wind to sail to Nevis. Graham had one of his panic sessions. His GPS was showing our anchor had slipped a few yards. No worries I thought we were at least 100 yards off the beach. Graham looked very scared and insisted on moving instantly. "What's the problem we can see the beach, we can see if the boat starts to move again" I said.

He was obviously very worried. So we up anchored and set sail back down the coastline to pick up the channel to open water before hitting the notorious South East Reef.

The wind was dead on our nose from the Southwest. First time since being here in the Caribbean that the wind has been from this direction. We motored all the 57 miles to Charlestown on Nevis. On the way we tried Larry again and this time he was man enough for the job. I was so pleased.

Arrived in Charlestown and its raining. The first time. I wonder if it's because we are further north. After seeing high cloud around the other mountainous islands of Saba and Eustatia I came to the conclusion they created their own eco climate. The buoys were much too far from the town so we moved nearer the towns harbour and dinghy dock which would be much better for the visit tomorrow morning.

We cruised around and found a nice space to moor not far from the dockside. Ideal.

Suddenly Graham had another panic attack and said we might drag in the night. Not again. I wanted to tell him to shut up but it's no good having a crew member panicking all night. I asked him in no uncertain terms why he hadn't mentioned his concerns earlier. Off we go again back to the original buoys two miles up the beach. It absolutely tipped it down.

Later we took the dinghy to the beach and Graham went off in a huff and Matthew, Barbara and I had a very pleasant lobster dinner at a famous yesteryear restaurant called Sunshine's.

The next morning we took the dinghy ashore again and went to sign in at Immigration and Customs. What a palavor. Some stuck up young official decided that he would throw the book at me. He said we should not under any circumstances moor the boat along the beach before clearing customs. What we should have done was moor the boat near the dockside on special yellow marked custom buoys. Only after clearing paperwork would we be allowed to moor somewhere else. He decided we would have to follow the rules. I pleaded that all the crew were touring the island and I couldn't move the boat on my own.

Eventually he relented, signed the papers and let me go. What a nasty individual. Why do they employ these little Hitler's? The continuous paperwork and clearing is bad enough without putting up with these sad power hungry dictators.

The tour next day was a delight. We (minus Graham) took a bus to Golden Rock Plantation Inn. Previously it was an old Colony sugar plantation. There were some old buildings still remaining and the rest had been lovingly restored. The views over the bay and the well kept gardens gave an almost believable feeling of being a plantation owner some 200 years ago. We left after a very nice but expensive Lobster sandwich.

Sailed up the coast of Nevis to Shitten Bay for lunch, then sailed on to Whitehouse Bay for the night. Before sunset we watched the pelicans diving and catching little fish. There was also lots of splashing around the boat as the big fish chased the little fish. Quite a commotion. A Booby bird sat on the pulpit and joined us for dinner.

Nearby was a very good pontoon and I wondered what it was doing in such a remote Bay. I found out later when Matthew and I went for a run around the Salt Pond. It was being transformed into a large lagoon complex presumably for a whole range of water activities. We saw a number of wild monkeys and picked up some very rare looking shells and a Conch shell that Matthew took back to the boat.

Next stop was St Kitts just a few miles further north. Port Zante Marina was very basic for such a busy port. Cold showers, different electricity and no gas refills. I took a taxi to a number of different Gas suppliers but none had camping gas. The electricity supply was now as the USA system with different Hertz cycles. I managed to buy a 30 Hz plug but was not at all confident that I could get the wiring right. There were some workmen close by and the electrician offered to do it for me. I gave him a beer while he scratched his head trying to solve getting the plug together correctly. He must have been a good hour but succeeded in solving the problem. I offered him some money but he refused outright. What a difference to the UK. It really struck me that not all people are so materialistic and money conscious.

That night we went for a meal and Graham recommended the Stone Wall Restaurant. It was a bit snobby but the food was good value. I suppose they get most of their clientele from the rich cruise boats that arrive daily. This port was purpose built for the big cruisers. Perhaps that's why the Marina was so poorly furnished. The town was seething with tourists. Not my cup of tea.

Although we had now had 3 days of rain off and on it didn't stop the flies and mosquitos. Everyone was suffering from bites to a greater or lesser degree. What a let down after Jolly Harbour Marina.

St Kitts is famous for its Forts. Brimstone Hill Fort is the best fortification in the West Indies. It made an interesting tour for us three. There were very good signs and information telling about the history. Despite its many guns and hilltop advantage the French succeeded in ousting the Brits. They bombarded the fort from the shoreline and then besieging the fort starving the people into submission.

The Navy surgeon's demonstration was very educational. He put to bed the old fallacy about getting drunk before amputation. This is the worst thing to do because the alchohol makes the heart beat faster and therefore resulting in a good deal of lost blood

During the return bus ride back to the port I noticed a familiar yacht moored outside in the Bay. It was Fair Encounter. That night we dined with John and Joyce. Graham was happy enough and Barbara appreciated the company of another woman. I was just happy to meet up with "old friends" again. It wasn't exactly Matthews's company however yet again he was chatty, polite and altogether a matured adult individual. I was very proud of him. He's been great company, almost like a best mate.

Easy going Eustatia .

It's the first Dutch owned island I have visited and once again there is a very distinct difference when the home country, in this instance Holland funds the cost of supporting vital infrastructure services. Good roads, drainage and an information centre with Internet services for instance.

I think the indigenous people want to remain as an annexe to Holland but might have a problem with the currency choice. It seemed silly and inefficient for such a small island to have their own currency. They do plan to convert to US Dollars soon.

The town is high above the sea with oil storage and pier further north.

Matthew and I took a walk up to Quill Volcano and could view the Pier below. It reminded me of Southampton or Harwich with so many tankers off loading and loading their oil. Quite a strange view for a remote island in the Caribbean.

This commercial business must be a hangover from the 19th century trading days when Eustatia offered tax free trading. This was a great boon to the English and French trading boats that had stiff customs taxes imposed on their own islands.

The walk to Quill Mountain was quite a trek as it is exposed to the sun for most of the journey. Barbara had ducked out for this very reason. On the way up we saw hundreds of crabs. I wondered how they lived on the side of a mountain and did they ever return to the sea? Once up the top there is a rough path which takes walkers down to the bottom of the Volcano. We decided it was just more of the same trees and vegetation and returned back down the mountain. A pleasant walk which had very few obstacles and took a couple of hours. A nice break from the confines of the boat.

Our anchorage was very rolly which made it difficult to sleep particularly as I had picked up 2 nasty bites and a long slash across my arm. I guess it must have been a jellyfish?

There's good snorkelling just of the beach in Gallows Bay it has quite a big depth change and Matthew caught a Remourer fish. They have a flat bottom side so they can succour themselves on the bigger fish such as sharks. Matthew saw one whilst snorkelling on the ledge coming up towards him but it soon swam away.

So Steep Saba

This is last of the small islands between Antigua and St Martin. It is also Dutch owned and part of the three Dutch colonies with St Martin being the third. We motored there and anchored in Wells bay which is a couple of miles up the coast. There was one very small gap in the rocky coastline where one could feasibly land the dinghy but the pilot book warned against the dangers. The sea was not so rolly even though there was a good swell around because of the relatively poor weather we had been experiencing. I say relatively but compared to Europe it was still lovely and warm and the rain showers didn't last long.

In the morning we went to Fort Bay and moored up for customs clearance. The marina was not really a marina. There wasn't a pier or pontoon and only two small bars and an information office for obtaining a touring ticket. I still had to check in and the information office lady who was from UK West Country was more than helpful but could'nt chase down the customs official. They are a world unto their own. What a pain.

She gave us a good rundown on the islands history and pointed out some of the places to snorkel in Saba which was supposed to be one of the best areas in the Caribbean. She also stated in no uncertain terms not to attempt to beach the dinghy when we return to Wells Bay. Even the locals are very careful not to land here unless the weather is absolutely right. Many touring boats had come to grief with fatalities.

Saba is only 3 miles square and extremely steep and high. The main town is almost at the top of the mountain and appropriately named The Bottom. Because there is very little transport on the island one has to hitch hike up from Fort bay to the town. It's not recommended to walk because it's so steep. It's the norm here to hitchhike.

Matthew and l visited the official Tourist Office and decided to qualify for their mountain climb certificate. This entailed walking up 1000 steps through dense tropical forest to the top 2864 feet above.

Beware of the final 200 feet. It's very slippery and requires scrambling over some big branches and rocks. We arrived with low cloud and mist surrounding the peak so the views weren't brilliant. The flora and fauna was excellent but still no parrots! On our way down to collect our certificates the sky cleared and we took some pictures of the town which was very pretty and well laid out.

In the morning I went to the customs office and completed the paperwork. As we returned to Wells Bay we could see the mooring buoys were already chocker - block and only one remaining. I told Graham to put his foot down to beat another yacht arriving a few yards away. After a few minutes the engine alarm started buzzing and the engine cut out. Quite a fright for me. I checked the engine and couldn't spot anything wrong. The impeller hadn't blown. Within a few minutes the engine cooled down and we started up again.

The delay meant we had to anchor between the moored boats in 15 metres with lots of chain out. After two attempts we were happy the anchor had gripped.

We were parked quite close to the north end of Wells Bay so a short dinghy ride to the snorkelling caves where we could moor alongside on special dinghy buoys. There was still a large swell and it was too rough to venture into the caves. Quite a disappointment.

Matthew caught 5 fish that day. It didn't surprise me with such bad smelling squid.

Suave St Barts

Our next stop included a pleasant sail to St Barts and the port of Gustava. It is a French colony very rich and very chic. The marina provides stern to mooring onto the quayside. We dropped anchor some 60 metres out and reversed back onto the quay which we completed very satisfactorily. House point for everyone. There was also a bit of a swell so springs are required together with a Pasarelle if possible. No electricity although the boxes were all installed. Hopefully the brisk wind will continue to charge Doris. The marina was very big with all the posh gin palaces moored on the opposite side close to all the restaurants and facilities.

The marina was integrated into the town so I soon found a place that provided replacement camping Gas bottles. It was a French town after all.

Spent the afternoon chilling out on Shell beach a ten minute walk away. The wind was perfect so I planned to return the next day with my windsurfing gear. It was populated with all the beautiful people. Young girls and boys presumably off work for the afternoon. Matthew was in his element and stayed on the beach after I left.

We all dined out together so Graham was happy. I was not. We returned to find the batteries were flat. I didn't leave any lights switched on so flat batteries were the verdict. The next morning I organised two new batteries at a cost of 300 Euros. This is an expensive Island.

I hired a taxi the next day and took my gear to Shell beach. By the time I had launched, the wind dropped a little and I just couldn't get going. Another guy swam out and tried his luck but also gave up. My windsurfing bad luck was annoying me.

The beach was nice and the views very charming with all the young dudes so not too upset.

That evening I told Barbara and Graham I wanted some more time with Matthew. Barbara was perfectly OK with this arrangement but Graham moaned and groaned about being on his own. What a spoilt brat he is.

We saw him later drinking with the crew of a large 100 foot yacht. He seemed in his element with so many guys to talk with and share sailing small talk. I half wished he would join them permanently. The next day I noticed the crew were part of the yacht parked next to us so Graham was on tender hooks when we left. He so wanted to leave with a good impression so when we went a bit close to their side he started panicking. They were all paid crew so what's all the big fuss I thought.

There is a very nice spot just around the side of St Barts so we stopped over for a night in St Colombier Bay. Then off to St Martin with a good 30+ easterly breeze.

22nd March. Seething St Martin

The Island is half Dutch and half French. Everyone speaks English so no problems with language. There are many marinas to choose from. I had the usual difficulties getting them on the radio. This has been a continuous problem throughout the Caribbean. I guess if need be they would all offer a mooring to yachts turning up unannounced but one cannot be too sure. I wanted to secure DwW on a pontoon because I was due to return for Jamie's wedding on the 24th March so security was important Barbara was also returning to the UK and Graham had said he was fixed up with other plans whilst I was away.

Simpson Bay seemed the best bet with at least 3 marinas situated inside the lagoon and bridge. We booked into Simpson Bay Marina after failing to raise any of the other cheaper marinas.

We arrived at 11.45 just 15 minutes after the bridge had closed. The next opening would be 17.30 so we skirted around the bay just outside. It was very busy with most of the mooring buoys occupied. I got the anchor ready but the windlass motor was playing up therefore little choice but to moor on one of the buoys closest to the beach. We approached very carefully indeed and measured 2.5 metres on the depth gauge. Hopefully the tide drop isn't too steep before we leave to enter Simpson Bay. Managed to get windlass motor running again after a good clean. The salt deposit out here is horrendous and requires constant checking of joints and connections electrical or otherwise.

We went through at 17.30, moored up and decided we are the smallest boat here. It's not cheap at 40 dollars a night but the facilities and location are excellent and the staff extremely helpful and without any fuss quickly supplied a 30 to 50 Hz converter for pontoon electricity.

The following day I changed the oil and oil filters after exceeding 50 engine hours. I have kept a very strict routine where the engine is concerned. Apart from the overheating in Saba, Ernie has performed magnificently.

The Beach was just across the road from the Marina. It is the same one that we moored in yesterday. I swam out just short of the buoy. I could stand up on the bottom. Whoops.

Had a great final night with Matthew. (no moans from Graham). Wonder why? We dined in Pineapple Pete's. Good value, good food and good music. One of the audience sang a Led Zeppelin song. It was almost better then the original.

24th March. Back to the UK

Departed boat after saying goodbye to Graham and also Barbara who was returning the next day. At the airport I had a few minutes to spare and logged onto the internet for any messages. There in front of my eyes in simple words was a message from Marcus saying he would not be returning as he had an offer of a contract starting in May which he couldn't refuse. I tried calling him but as expected he was on voicemail. I didn't want to leave a message for such a serious matter and tried many times to catch him whilst we waited for the flight. I was at the end of my tether. I finally left a message for Marcus explaining how difficult it would be to get a replacement at such a late stage and if finance was a problem to get back to me ASAP.

He never did. This was not a good time for celebrating my son's wedding. I felt so lonely and inadequate.

The flight back was not altogether straight forward. We had to change for the Virgin flight at Antigua so it was important that the local Liat flight made the connection. While we waited and the attendant informed us that our flight had been delayed but would get us there in plenty of time. Then they asked us if we would wait for the next flight which didn't stop at St Kitts and would arrive at or by the same time as our original flight. I declined but they then said our seats had already been allocated to two passengers in St Kitts. We didn't have much choice.

We eventually arrived with 45 minutes left to book in to Virgin. A stressful time but it stopped me from worrying about the boat. We were concerned that Customs at Antigua would scupper our check in. On arrival there was a sign directing us to bypass customs and a trolley man was waiting for us. In ten minutes since landing we were on the end of a short remaining queue for the UK flight.

To hell and back

As soon as I got home Barbara rang from the boat. She had just left and informed me that Graham had also packed his bag. I said to Barbara he was joining another boat whilst I was away. "No he isn't, he tells me he booked his UK return ticket back in St Barts" she replied. Why, oh why didn't he have the decency or guts to tell me? Something about his concerns over unqualified crew so Barbara was informed.
Can it get any worse I thought? I tried to look on the positive side and decided that perhaps it was for the best with his condescending and patronising attitude to everyone on board. Not to mention his extremely poor communication skills. Good riddance is what I say.

I was having difficulty getting into Jamie's wedding celebrations with the crew problems in the back of my mind. We met that Saturday to watch Crystal palace play. Hope they stave off relegation. It was such a pleasure to have Matthew and Jamie together. My nephew Mark joined us as he's a converted Man Utd to Palace supporter.He's found the true and righteous supporters path. Such a nice guy. Tina his mum should be very proud of him.

So back home and time to review my options for sailing back to the UK. Received quote for shipping DwW back. 8700 Euros. Apart from the high cost I was now absolutely determined to return with the boat so option A went out of the window. Option B involves paying crew to bring the boat back. I contacted a delivery skipper based in Portsmouth. He was very helpful and said he could get another two crew who would pay their own costs. His bill would be £3000.00 for a 40 day all in package. The offer was very tempting especially as he would give me a bit of a rest and less worry after my 12 months skippering. I posted an advert on the World cruising club site but didn't hold out much hope. They had already intimated that getting crew to come back to the UK was not easy because unlike coming across here nobody wanted to return.

I hired Alan the next day and posted a 'crew wanted' advert on crew seekers to cover the Tortola to UK trip. I also rang around to get a feel for crew. To my relief within a couple of days was pretty well fixed up.
Chris who had been pencilled in since we left Gran Canaria rang me and we exchanged one or two of his concerns, namely that his wife had been worried on his ARC passage since they lost their Iridium phone after the first few days. I assured Chris that on DwW we had full sat phone service

for the whole 2700 miles and also that I was a net controller with a good SSB radio. This made his wife happy and he signed up for the return trip.

Hamish filled the last slot. He's an Australian and owns his own boat moored in Southampton. His had just given up his job to concentrate on preparing his boat to sail to Australia with his young wife. He wanted to get the confidence and experience of completing a major ocean passage. His plan was to sail with us to the Azores and then return to complete fitting out for his own boat. This fitted in well with a friend of mine based in Shoreham who wanted to complete the Azores to UK passage.
That Sunday Cara and her partner Steven came for lunch. St Martin and the boat seemed a long, long way away.

I was now feeling much better but still had one remaining challenge. I wanted to finish Step 6 which meant getting the boat to the BVI's for the remaining 3 weeks cruise. Marilyn a sailing friend from the UK was due to join the boat in Tortola. So I needed someone to crew from St Martin to Tortola. Alan suggested we set off from St Martin but I was set on the BVI's.

The Coconut Man cometh

Alan recommended a contact in St Martin that might help me get the boat to the BVI's. I emailed him but he was already in Tortola and would have to fly back. I got the impression he wasn't really interested. The Simpson Bay marina staff hadn't come up with anything either. Then I received an email via the WCC website. A Dr Stanimar wanted to join me for the trip. He sent me his CV which to say the least was strange. He had spent the last 6 months in an Ecuador jungle researching and recording teak tree locations for which he had a GPS. This was the extent of his sailing skills apart from some dinghy sailing on the Black Sea 30 years ago. He was a qualified Doctor in Dentistry but gave it up many years ago in Bulgaria. He sent me a picture showing him dressed up in a smart white suit and white hat. What was I letting myself in for? I had one main concern. Was he gay? "No, certainly not" he said. I found out later that he was a widower and his wife had been schizophrenic. She had inherited a restaurant that she was unable to run so she advertised for a husband with very strict conditions:

1. Did not smoke
2. Was a doctor
3. Not married
4. Completed University degree

There were a couple more ticks required but I can't remember them. Anyway Stan got all the ticks and entered into a contractual marriage. From all accounts he managed to get all the restaurant debts written off due to his wife's illness and sell the business at a fair profit.

I signed him up and he thanked me for the opportunity, promising to take me for a lobster lunch when I returned to St Martin.

He said he had ordered 20 coconuts for the trip. I was in no position to argue.

So things looked good for a full crew and "Stan" to help me complete the sixth step to heaven with some training and good guidance.

The Deserters

I sent an email to Marcus saying thanks for letting me down so badly and I would see him in court on my return to the UK. He had caused me to have to employ a delivery skipper and the loss of the ARC Europe entry fee. The ARC Europe trip would add another 10 days to the passage and therefore a further £750 crew cost to the journey. I had asked Graham when I left to check the electrics on the boat. He hadn't the decency to do that for me. I'm glad the way things have turned out and I don't have to suffer his continuous moaning.

These past events first with my stepfather and then Marcus and Graham had really knocked my confidence. A year ago I would have just shrugged them off.

I hope the Marina staff is keeping an eye on things.

I finally made a note to get better weather reporting facilities for our return trip. Now that we are not joining the ARC Europe we will need to be more independent of weather predictions.

My son gets married

It's the 2nd April and Jamie meets us at the The Bedford Hotel. That evening the entire family meet for a meal and Cara wants to split the bill as she didn't have any drinks.

My boat days come flooding back regarding all the fuss about crew eating out and wanting to work every fine detail out before splitting and paying the bill. I expressed my frustration and she was really upset. I was surprised how she had 'tapped in' to my state of mind.

Back at the hotel I had to eat humble pie and apologise that I didn't realise how worried she was about finances.

The wedding was a great success. (Jamie's bride) Helen's parents doted on their only daughter and spared not a penny of expense. They are very loving and marvellous parents. The Church service included a choir and church bells. The Hotel laid on a 5 course meal for 120 guests and everything went like clockwork. Helen's mum is a head teacher and her military precision planning ensured total success. All the speeches were excellent and obviously well rehearsed. Jamie said I didn't have to get up and speak - I think he knew I was not exactly on top form. But I had spent some time during the trip preparing and after a bit of confusion as to whether the Bridegrooms father should be speaking I delivered my words. To this day I don't know how it went. The audience seemed impressed but wedding days are always so positive aren't they.

It was so nice just to see all the family and relations on such a happy occasion.

I had a few days back at the house pottering around, mowing the lawn and planting the seed beans in the allotment. I took my usual run along to Lancing and was pleasantly surprised that I could sprint back to Shoreham between each Groyne. It was very therapeutic and making it hard to turn my thoughts to St Martin and the long trip back.

The goodbyes were quite emotional which is very out of character for Diane and me. We shared mixed emotions concerning the remainder of the trip and despite it being the last leg and a final return to the UK we both knew there was some 4000 miles to go across the North Atlantic.

The flight back was uneventful but my mind was racing with thoughts of how to handle Step Seven to Heaven. Then on my way through Antigua airport I spotted John and Joyce of Fair Encounter. They were meeting their family to join them on their boat moored up in English harbour. Meeting them after sharing the same adventure seemed to be a good omen for me, but sad that I wouldn't be joining them on the ARC Europe passage.

Getting ready for the final leg

Stan met me at the airport. He looked very strange in his white suit and white fedora. It was almost surreal but I took a liking to him instantly despite his very average grasp of English. He was very keen and excited to be joining the boat and encouraged me no end because here was someone I could teach the bare basics and know he would get on with it and not moan. So far so good.

DwW was very tidy and shipshape. Thank you Barbara. The next two days I spent teaching Stan all the basics to sail the boat. He was an excellent student listening and writing things down. He had a curious diet which consisted mainly of raw food such as red peppers goats' cheese and dry bread. This diet was as a result of living in the jungle for 6 months and not being able to cook hot food. His luxury was one coconut per day. He expounded on the merits of coconut oil and the roughage of the white coconut. Funny how he liked white things so much?

We managed to find time in the afternoon to visit the beach and swim. Stan wouldn't go any earlier due to the strength of the sun's rays. He hated the cold climate of Europe, loved the warm climate of the Caribbean yet kept himself plastered in sun tan oil and protective clothing. He explained that skin care and protection was of the utmost importance living in the jungle.

10th April BVI here we come

I took Stan off to the police station which doubled up as a customs offices located just over the bridge and kept my fingers crossed. Lets face it I didn't know a lot of his background and a Bulgarian with an Austrian passport was rather out of the ordinary. It was fine and Stan on the way out pointed to the cheap Lobster stand next door. "Very smashing good cheap lobster here" he said.

We returned to the Marina, two frogmen turned up and in a couple of hours completely scrubbed the bottom of the boat next door. How much for DwW I asked. "75 euros" came the reply. So the next morning they give her a nice clean bottom. Well worth the money since a lot of stuff was collecting underneath. It had been 14 months since the anti - fouling was last applied and was obviously breaking down rapidly.

The wind had been quite strong the past few days but never higher than low 30's.

We are as ready as we will ever be and set off to sail via Anguilla. It took us 6 hours with the final two hours heading into the wind. So on with Larry who wasn't very happy dealing with 30 knots of wind pushing the bow from left and right. Stan had his first go at helming. He was all over the place. It turns out he has never driven a car in his life so a wheel and steering was all alien to him.

I was not fazed. At least he wasn't seasick but he did spend a lot of the 6 hours hanging onto the mast. Even more important he was such good company and a great conversationalist. He had picked up a smattering of Spanish whilst in Ecuador and could speak the language better than I so we shared one or two hours over the days speaking some very basic Spanish. I was so pleased with him and such a difference to Graham.

We anchored up in Anguilla and Stan was full of joy and excitement. A good day.

We anchored in Little Bay for the night. Real shame we didn't have time to explore the island it looks absolutely beautiful.

We planned to leave 2pm the next day. Based on an average of 5 knots we should hit BVI's some 80 miles distance early the next morning. Fingers crossed for Larry but not optimistic with 30+ knots of wind. Set off with small reefed Genoa and still managing 5+ knots speed. Stan was learning quickly and during the night we worked together very well handling a nasty gust. Larry was performing well which was a great relief. But the journey was tiring with just the two of us and I was glad to see the gap between Round Rock and Ginger Island appear on the horizon at 7 am. The gap looked very narrow and I was a little confused until as usual close up all becomes clear. We were both tired and pleased to get a good anchorage next to Virgin Gorda (fat women in Hisponola) outside Spanish Town Marina in St Thomas Bay.

Slept for 12 hours solid before getting up and taking the dinghy to Spanish Town.

Custom's calamity again.

Found the customs office and mistakenly said we arrived yesterday. That set the fox among the pigeons. "You should have cleared yesterday" said the officer. He was very angry and left us to wait for another customs officer who was friendlier. This clearance business is the bane of my life. The town is not that large but good for provisions.

Spent the rest of the day on the beach. Stan spotted a coconut tree and that was it. He spent the next hour fixing up a long pole to knock the coconuts off the tree. He eventually succeeded and took great pride taking them aboard to replenish his dwindling stocks. He also repaired our very ragged flags. Sewing is a passion and hobby of his. I started thinking of other sewing jobs I could line up. There were many. Finally I ordered a couple of retaining pins for Doris and left a message for Mo to say that a package would be with her before she left the UK.

We sailed on down to find a good Marina near the capital of Tortola which is Road Town Harbour. Once again I couldn't get anyone on the blower except for the Burt Hotel marina. I had already studied the pilot book and thought this marina could be a problem for depth under the hull. I reserved a mooring but kept trying on the VHF. A young lady came on the blower from BVI Charters in Jome Marina. She guided us in past the Cruise dock. The marina had nice hot showers, water, electrics and very close to a couple of big supermarkets. This could be the place to prepare for the big trip.

Mo joins the boat

I took a taxi to the airport which as the crow flies isn't far but the road winds around a number of headlands. Yet a bill of 48 Dollars seemed very excessive. Mo wasn't impressed. We spoke about Stan as she would be sharing the next couple of weeks with the both of us. Mo's reaction was one of "he seems very strange, will he be alright".

I reassured her that I had spent two weeks with him and although he had some strange ideas on food and people he was thoroughly genuine had a philosophical outlook and someone I could truly trust. Mo was not convinced because he dressed funny but I meant what I said because Stan was just this. A smashing bloke, unconventional which he certainly was but she wasn't prepared to see the inner man.

I find women quite fascinating. They seem to have this fatal attraction for the 'knight in shining armour' character which inevitably leaves them in tears and disappointment. Why can't they settle for a man with good common sense, perhaps a bit boring but good, upstanding and reliable? Its all way above my head how women see the opposite sex.

Back to the mundane duties around the boat. With the Duogen I fitted the pin that Mo brought with her but it was too short to go through the prop shaft. I spoke to Duogen and they said their supplier had delivered hundreds of pins all perfectly OK. They had a problem believing me until I tried the second one. It fitted perfectly and was a little longer than the faulty one. They were sympathetic and promised to send a replacement.

Just to add more frustration Diane had rang to say we were short of funds so I had spent the last two weeks on and off trying to cash in some American shares. I cannot begin to describe how difficult this was proving to be. American company personnel (specifically in this instance Smith Barney) are so polite and helpful but incredibly lacking in common sense and intuition. To cut a long story short I gave up trying to get around their bureaucracy and swore never to invest in foreign shares ever again.

Our first stop for the grand BVI tour was Marina Cay which on paper looked superb and an easy approach as long as one spots and heads for the red buoy Unfortunately it was chock-a-block with catamarans and charter boats with a mooring fee of 25 dollar's so we left early the next day for North Sound. A lovely lagoon but still very windy. The passage looks a bit foreboding but again very simple once there, providing one keeps inside the buoyed channel until the third red bouy when the whole lagoon and sailing area opens up. We could have turned right and anchored in Blunder Bay but we played safe and dropped anchor off Prickly Pear Island near Vixen Point very close to the Beach. I could see my long promised place called Bitter End just across the lagoon. Stan was busy repairing the sun canopy which was well past its sell date but he was not to be deterred.

We moved over to the Bitter End in the morning, filled up with fuel and water and moored on a buoy. We took the dinghy and planned to spend a few hours enjoying this famous place. Mo was keen to get some rays for her tan and sat beside a couple of American girls. One had her leg bandaged up and she had lots of bruising. It turns out that she went for a swim in the 'The baths' bay the day before and a strong wave swept through the famous round rocks and pushed her onto the rough rocks alongside. I was surprised that this location was a problem as it's well advertised as the place to see in the BVI's.

The wind was favourable and out comes the windsurfing gear. Once again too many boats and too many holes in the wind. Then a dinghy pulls alongside. Instantly I recognised Glenn from my last days in Lagos. It was then that he recommended Bitter End and to him it was his home. He was anchored off Saba Rock. He didn't recognise me at first and spotted me as a fellow windsurfer in the wrong place. He gave me a tow out of the harbour area just north of Saba rock and left me to my own devices. I had some good wind but didn't want to venture too far away because of unknown tides. That night we moved the boat up to a mooring off Saba Rock and joined Glenn for a meal in his favourite restaurant. He was no stranger here and knew all the locals. As usual Stan ate on the boat. This was not seen as a slight because I now knew that Stan hated noise and peoplc. He would run a mile from any place no matter how quiet. So Mo and I had a nice couple of hours with Glenn.

The food was good value and the scallops very nice. Of course Mo had taken to him at first sight. Well, I mean he was tall, handsome, and had his own boat. What more does a women want?

Whilst on the subject of desirable men, Mo spotted Necker Island on the way into the lagoon and drooled over her hero Richard Branson. So top of her stop offs was Necker. She spent the next couple of days finding out how we could get to visit the Island. I wasn't too keen neither was Stan but it was

Mo's holiday. Apparently one has to book the private villa to visit and only when it's not occupied can you have a chance of a day's visit.

This would entail contacting the maitre d'or and getting permission. Also I had studied the chart and it looked as though we need to plan very carefully our approach and anchorage.

As it turned out the timing wasn't quite right for us to visit the island and to sail to Anegada.

I can't say the same for their mooring buoys. The next morning we set off for Anegada and to my horror found the mooring rope 90% cut through caused by a rusty eye on the buoy. We could quite easily have come loose in the night and ended up crashing through the numerous boats moored in Bitter End.

18th April Next stop Anegada

Excellent sail registering 6 to 7 knots boat speed all the way. Maybe the clean bottom gave us a bit more speed. Hope it stays that way for the trip home.

The island is surrounded by the Anegada Reef and has a very low promontory of only 28 metres height but we steered well clear of Pelican Point on the south east of the island and headed towards the red marker just outside of Setting Point Bay further along the coast. Spot red buoys at 90 degrees to the left and it's an easy approach. The sand is soft so good anchoring and plenty of mooring buoys.

Clearance was not a problem. There was just one friendly official who did both immigration and customs.

It's quite a long island with a large reservoir in the middle. They boast of flamingos but I got the feeling they would be hard to track down and we only had the one day free. We hired three bikes and set off for Loblolly Bay. I wanted to see the Iguana Research Centre near the capital town called The Settlement whilst Stan carried on to the Bay.

It wasn't much to see. Just a few small Iguanas and the town had just a few shops. The whole island's population is only 200 or so people

By the time we reached Loblolly Bay we had cycled at least 8 miles so Mo was rather tired. The trip was well worth it. A superb location with masses of reef some 50 yards off the beach. I swam out and saw some excellent coral fish. On the way back a 4 foot Barracuda swam alongside. They are a very inquisitive fish and not at all dangerous.

Stan was no where to be seen. He was off on one of his coconut jaunts with my windsurfing mast with a sharp knife tied on the end.

He finally turned up along the beach carrying two large sacks full of coconuts. I went to help him and asked how he was going to cycle back with the equivalent of two bags of cement. No problem for him he was going to walk back pushing the bike for the 6 miles.

He was so elated and satisfied at having discovered and collected so many coconuts.

Mo and I cycled off agreeing to meet Stan in one of the lobster restaurants later that evening.

The island is famous for its lobsters. Every place serves them fresh. We chose a restaurant after much fussing. Mo was keen to eat at Neptune's but it was full up so we ended up further down the bay in The Lobster Trap. It was a warm night and 10 knots of wind so we sat outside waiting for Stan to arrive.

In the meantime Mo didn't like the wind and the lobster order was not correct so the cook was not happy. Not one of my best lobster nights out especially as I had forgotten to put on insect bite spray, which resulted in a lot of scratching and itching.

To my amazement Stan arrived complete with his coconut catch. He hadn't hitched a lift and walked all the way back. I was mightily impressed. Mo was non plussed and thought he was mad.

Back to the BVI's

We set off the next day to sail back to Cane Gardens which was recommended in all the brochures as the hidden treasure of the BVI's. It was a bit too commercialised for me. I think Anegada had spoilt us and I still have fond memories of all the deserted islands last visited. Still it had a nice beach and all the facilities.

Mo expressed her interest in visiting Brewers Bay as a friend had recommended it. I said we couldn't because there was no where to anchor. Was this fact or fiction????

The evening ashore was another restaurant fiasco. Mo spent all her time reserving a table which was completely unnecessary and I spent my time keeping Stan and Mo happy. It seems strange now but small things like organising trips back to the boat in the dinghy get very difficult and cause frictions. Tonight was just such an occasion. Mo and Stan ended up arguing about getting back to the boat. I took them back and spent the rest of the evening enjoying a few beers on my own. I will have to apologise to Mo for not being more sympathetic to her needs however inconsequential they may be. Perhaps I am a bit short tempered what with the hot nights, restless legs and its getting close to the big trip home.

We next visited Jost van Dyke Island and anchored off Great Harbour. This time we did experience a nice meal but not cheap. The venue was Foxy's Bar which is quite famous. Similar to The Bitter End I think these famous places are better known by the Americans. This would fit in with the whole area which is almost 100% American charter boats and holidaymakers.

The evening adventure didn't end there. As I prepared the dinghy I accidentally kicked Mo's 'very expensive' sandals off the pontoon. What a palaver. It was like the end of the world. Luckily with the help of a local we managed to retrieve them.

Hidden Treasure

With no wind to speak of we motored onto our next destination, Norman Island. Lots of boats so very busy which meant we had to take a mooring near the Party time boat in the SE corner of the bay. Lots of noise and high decibels. Won't come here again. On the funnier side Mo spotted a German boat just across from us, which isn't unusual you would think, then I noticed that they were all stark naked. On close inspection a women was standing on the bow swinging around the front stay just like a pole dancer but without the figure and graces. Not a pretty sight. Then we ran out of water. We had plenty of fresh drinking water but the tanks were empty so no more showers until we return to Tortola.

We took the dinghy out and around the bay to Treasure Point which is a good place for snorkelling in the underwater caves. Despite the many boats it did provide some very nice snorkelling. Stan joined me for his very first dive and was overwhelmed with the experience. It was also a historical place due to an old story that a certain Pirate named Captain Hawkins buried his treasure on the island and never managed to return after being killed. For some reason Stan was very enthusiastic about this area and dressed up in his best white attire to have some pictures taken. He tried very hard to convince me to sign up to his idea for a treasure hunt. He explained that we could hire a helicopter and through extensive satellite tracking and photographing the land we could spot where the treasure was located underground. I just nodded and went with the flow.

We were also joined by Fair Encounter so I dinghied over and gave them the ARC Europe flags that were entrusted with me to hand out in Nanny Cay marina, Tortola. I was glad they were in a hurry to leave as I felt a pang of envy and sad that we would not be accompanying them back to the UK.

Single handed sailing must be simpler

Sopers Hole was a pleasant enough place with plenty of facilities for shopping and eating. Popular place for the American charter boats. Had another repeat of 3 people all with different priorities. Mo wants to get back to the boat, Stan wants to Internet and I am happy supping a beer watching a local on the quay trying to catch one of the 4foot barracudas swimming around for throw away scraps. Single handed sailing would solve this problem of dinghy use.

Last "port of call"

We tacked up to Coopers Island on a pleasant beam reach and moored up in Machiereil Bay. A very nice location quiet and peaceful. Mo and I took the dinghy to the dinghy dock and as she clambered over the front of the dinghy she fell into the water. A wet and shocked Mo climbed onto the pontoon with a hang dog expression and blamed me for not holding the dinghy close to the pontoon. Flipping cheek. I now look back with amusement and a little chuckle.

All in all the BVI tour has been a lovely adventure and I was so glad I made the effort to come rather than stay in St Martin. My story may sound all doom and gloom with dinghy management and other problems but they were minor events when taken in light of all the beautiful Islands and locations in this vast area. It certainly stands up to its reputation for one of THE best sailing and cruising locations in the world. The consistent f4 winds, warm seas and blue skies make it a perfect charters paradise.

It's now the 26th April and we complete an easy downwind sail back to the marina in Road Town. I quickly glance over to "The Baths" on Virgin Gorda wishing we had stopped off there. But time is once again against us.
So here we are in Jome marina once again. It was certainly nice to have a shower after three days with empty tanks. Noticed Adrianna a UK Cruiser in Dock. Wonder if it's due to return to the UK?
Time to give the boat a good clean and find out where to get the gas bottles filled for the trip home. I had tried to say to Mo that she needs to help clean the boat properly and clean the linen but she wanted to do the island tour so muggins here together with Stan's help were left to do most of the work and visit the laundry. Ah well, she was on her well earned holiday. Stan had just about stitched every piece of rope end and loose canopy strands. A grand job indeed. Spoke to our neighbours a Norwegian boat returning all the way back to Norway. They are leaving tomorrow with the High Azores looking established and providing fair weather. Mo and I took the dinghy over to Village cay marina for her last night. We spoke about my trip to Australia

and joining my son Jamie for Xmas. It was the third time I had told her. Surely my conversation isn't so boring that she can't remember the first two times?

Mo took the taxi back rather than return by dinghy in the dark. I think her experience on Norman Island had left its mark.

I will always remember Mo when I think of the BVI's and The Bitter End. Mo always nagged me to make sure I didn't make the coffee grounds Bitter by pouring boiling hot water on them.

All change again

Mo departs for the UK. New crew arrive and usual strained introductions as we get to know one another. Alan gets to grips with apparent boat inadequacies and seems very well informed. Overall crew seem very good which augers well for the big trip.

Let's get ready

Early rise next day Alan suggested Stan should join us because with 5 crew we can have a "Mother's Day" watch. This simply means that every fourth day one crew member has the day off boat sailing duties does nothing but cooking cleaning and general welfare of the other crew.

Stan was due to leave the boat today and his attempts to crew on another boat either from here or Fort Lauderdale had proved completely fruitless owing to his lack of sailing experience. Needless to say he was absolutely thrilled when I invited him to join us for the trip to the UK.

We planned the provisioning whilst Alan organised the boat for the return journey. He was not a fan of the twin headsail set up especially going back to the UK. So he set about changing the sails for a more traditional arrangement. We organised the running rigging to ensure we would be able to easily put the pole up for goosewinging the main and Genoa.

We had our first of many discussions about the merits of twin headsails instead of goose winging but he insisted he could sail as fast with his set up rather than the twin headsails which he thought could cause a Chinese jibe so were dangerous.

We never did agree on this matter.

The afternoon was spent buying provisions from the local supermarkets which were nicely placed to the marina. Costs were not so nice and I was pleased with Stan's continuing positive attitude. It was obvious that his meagre provisions of dry bread, raw peppers, salted cod and goat's cheese were far cheaper than our more extravagant meats, cereal, and expensive pre-prepared foods. He never flinched when we split the bill 5 ways (even on the next shopping trip which totalled over 1500 dollars).

Hamish was busy using his electronics and engineering adeptness to fix one or two minor faults on the boat. One such fault was the engine revs counter which had never worked since I bought the boat. He simply dismantled it and reconnected the wires.

Not so simple was the saloon wiring. The middle lights had not worked since St Lucia. He took the panelling off and discovered the wires had been severely burnt and had shorted out. Quite a serious find as the wood was scorched and there was no telling what might happen in the future. 4 hours later he had cut out the offending wires and managed to repair most of the Saloon lights. I was mightily impressed with his skills.

Two days of preparing and we are ready for the off.

May 1st Seventh Step to Heaven – Back across the Atlantic and Home

Jome Marina, Road Town, Tortola

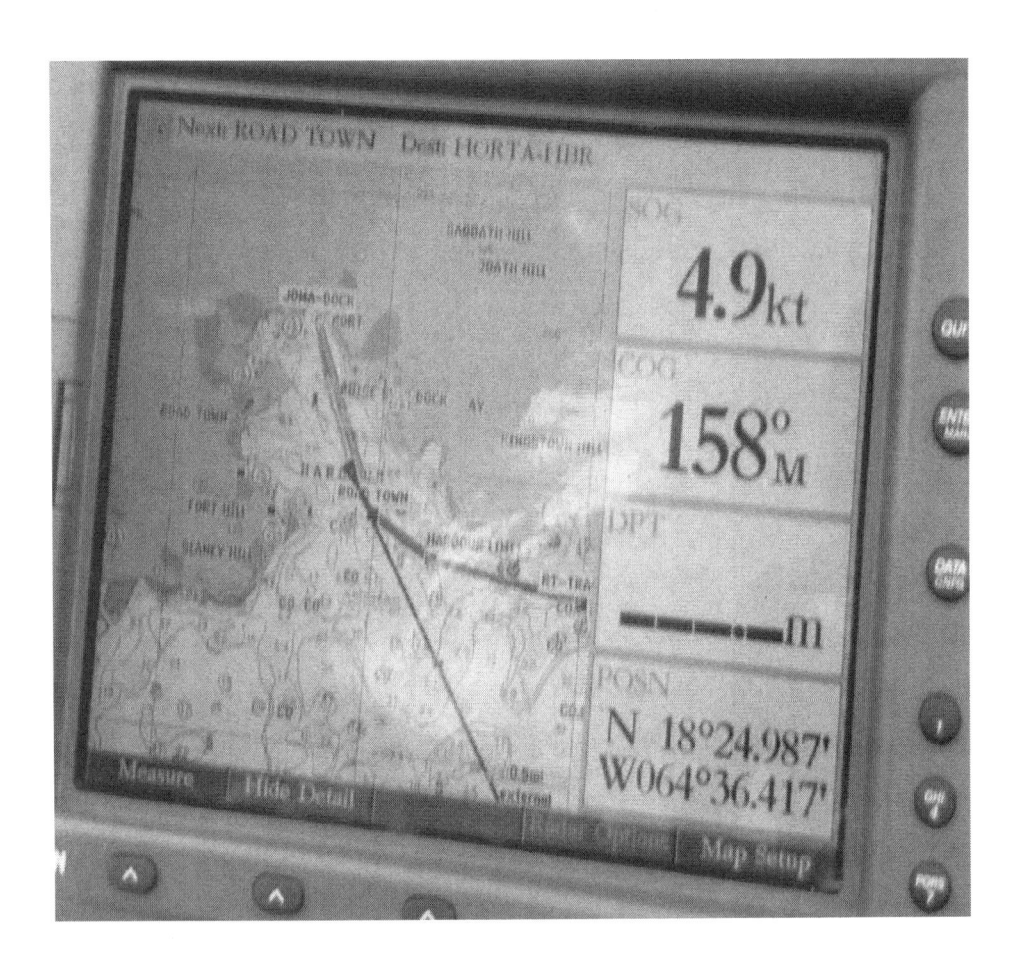

We departed with typical F4 winds and everyone prepared including Alan who had passed the boat to his satisfaction. My thoughts were on the weather across the big Atlantic. What conditions would we have to endure? Would they be in the right direction?

Would DwW continue to be so good and capable in bad conditions? I'm glad I hired Alan he's a good teacher and appears very well versed in passage making. He has a very accurate barometer and some good weather reporting software. This is going to be crucial without the backup of the ARC organisation which was so useful coming over here.

If we can achieve 100 miles per day average without serious incidents I will be a very happy man. Fingers crossed and pray to God. Wait a minute I'm not a religious man!

May 2nd Change of Plan

Our plan to sail direct to the Azores was not looking good. The more reliable NE winds were not what we wanted and Alan's hope of heading straight across the triangle to the Azores was not going to work. I had tried to tell him that DwW was not good at holding a close wind sail. It was plain to see that with a NE wind we would eventually end up halfway down the West African Coast! After 100 miles of sailing we had only crept 58 miles towards our destination. We had no option but to take the more traditional route to Bermuda, 800 miles further north, where we had a better chance of picking up the more favourable trade winds over to the Azores.

May 3rd - 4th Better direction

Our decision to go via Bermuda was proving correct. With a Northerly heading and an ENE wind we were making excellent progress and managed 144 miles on the second day. Chris managed to crack his nose whilst trying to fix a loose Babystay but generally everyone was getting into their routine with salt and sweaty bodies especially Stan's sleeping bag. I'm glad he opted for the forward cabin. He didn't complain about sharing the cabin with the provisions or about the water leaking through the windlass on deck. He didn't complain and just got on with fixing the problem himself with whatever material he could find. He's a good guy to have on board despite his lack of sailing skills. Other attributes make up for his lack of knowledge. The weather was looking pretty well settled so we had time to sort out a proper working weather reporting system. My plan was to ask Chris and Barbara back in the UK to send me Grib files based on my email to them giving our co-ordinates. But their files were far too large for the Mailasail software package. We used a combination of the Mailasail Gribfile download and a package called Viewfax which accepted the Gribfile data and gave us a printout with the boats position.

May 5th – 7th. We enter Bermuda High

With 500 miles remaining we enter the centre of the Bermuda high which might add further days to our crossing. Hamish is on a tight schedule to fly out of the Azores and Ian might have to wait around in the Azores also. Here we go again with crew priorities coming into the equation.

The engine is now on and routine very boring. It's getting noticeably colder, so sad to be leaving the warm blue cloudless skies. Tried some fishing but no good. Watched a film on the PC. Very strange sensation to be in the middle of the Atlantic completely enveloped in a fantasy world. My restless legs are a real nuisance. Hard to get to sleep and its much colder at night with damp also.

8th May. The last leg to Bermuda

Engine off at last after 40 hours. 100 miles remaining to St Georges harbour. Looks like we will arrive in the daylight which is no bad thing as the coast around the island has lots of reefs and hazards and the approach is a challenge. We found the Bermudan coastguard extremely helpful. They have a very strong signal that picks up boats within a 50 mile radius. Nevertheless we took a great deal of care approaching the entrance which was quite narrow.

Finally in side we experience a very large lagoon with little or no mooring pontoons but were fortunate to moor up alongside a big French catamaran that had ignored the local radio contact and just moored alongside a large concrete jetty reserved for large visiting boats of substantial size. Later we saw other boats trying to moor alongside the jetty further along .It had a sloping side that was hidden under water and made for very difficult mooring. I was surprised at the lack of facilities for such a well known Island and sailing venue. There were no electrics or water available.

Is this England?

Our first meal ashore was in The White Horse. It had English league football showing and was just like an English pub. We sat down to eat and I fell asleep eating my meal. The strains of the last week were showing.
The town was very quaint and similar to English Harbour. It certainly had a colonial feel to it with a set of stocks on the square. It was also a very special day to celebrate the arrival of the ship Deliverance 400 years ago. The expedition from England had floundered in very bad weather and ended up in Bermuda instead of Norfolk Virginia. The procession enacted the whole story of the brave seafarers and their passengers.

Later the Deliverance set sail and relieved the inhabitants of Jamestown on the mainland of North America and awarded recognition for their efforts. It was quite a realistic scene with actors playing back history on the Deliverance look-alike now standing in St Georges.

9th - 10th May final preparations for The Azores passage which is 1800 miles. The Bermudians are very friendly and helpful but also out to make a large profit from being the only port of call for hundreds of miles. Cost of food, fuel and water is astronomical. But we had no choice. To top it all they charged us 40 dollars a night to raft up to another boat without any access to water, showers or electricity. What a rip-off.

The weather predictions were not particularly good showing a number of lows coming down from the USA eastern seaboard. We would need to keep a close watch on these developing lows and ensure we stay well south of them.

11th May. We refuelled and waved goodbye to Starfire, a 27 ft Sadler from Fowey. This boat manned by two young guys had crossed our path both in Madeira and St Lucia after they had been supported by Silver Bear during the ARC crossing when they had to complete the Atlantic with a jury rudder. I admired their bravery in such a small boat.

11th May - Back to passage making and the long trip to the Azores. Very big swell and continuous monitoring of Grib reports to ensure we keep south of the approaching Lows. Joined by a large pod of dolphins at least 40. Stan is eating more of our food. Perhaps he's tiring of peppers, salt fish and dry bread.

12th May. Not much wind and engine on. A couple of maintenance jobs but other than this a pretty normal passage, sent an email to Terry wishing him a happy birthday. A bit boring really but boring means no problems which is fine by me. SW wind came back in the night.

13th May. Despite our best route planning tactics we didn't manage to miss the first Low. Took 20 hours to blow through. Gusting 55 knots so not a very pleasant night. Got a bit of a drenching. Come back Caribbean- all is forgiven. Larry and Doris both doing a grand job. Fingers crossed for 2nd Low coming through on Saturday night.

14th May. Lovely calm day after the Low. Everyone relaxed and happy. Put up downwind sailing that Alan had configured with traditional main and Genoa goose winged. We had to change the pole over every time we went from starboard to port heading. I wish I had been more insistent on keeping with our original twin headsail setup coming over with the ARC. It would have saved keeping on changing the pole from side to side. Larry decided to fall apart. Strange how all the securing screws on the wheel had worked loose?
The 2nd Low looked very active and so we headed further south to avoid the worst. Hope it doesn't also decide to move more south.

15th May. You guessed right. The Low did decide to track further south which bought us another very rough night of consistent winds in the 40's. As usual DwW took it all in her stride. What a great boat. Larry not happy with rough conditions and the Chart plotter fused. Fortunately I had another 3 amp fuse. These faults are expected in rough weather so pleased overall and crew happy enough and very competent. So pleased after the horrible

Graham times. Big swells and things keep moving all over the place. Dolphins join us for the third day running.

16th May. Light winds but maintaining good speed. Dolphins are here again and we nearly run down a turtle. Wonder if he's on the way to the Irish Sea? Quiet night and hopeful for some decent weather.

17th May. Caught up with Starfire. Spent a few hours taking some excellent pictures of each other. Minerva, a rather nice 65 foot Farr caught up with us early evening. Had difficulty with downwind sailing. Only wished we had twin headsail setup in place.

Not a very good night on watch but Chris spotted a whale first thing in the morning. It came within 30 yards of the boat. What a size and presence.

18th May. Starfire overtook us in the night. A 27 foot Sadler. No good at all a 27 foot boat going faster than us. Fresh food all gone so Vegetarian Hamish cooks us veggie meal. Kept farting. Very tempted to open whisky bottle to celebrate halfway stage but declined after feeling guilty about breaking passage making rule on non alcohol.

19th May. 49 years to the day my father died. I dwelt on thoughts of what he might have said and thought about my achievements here in the Atlantic Ocean 1800 miles from home. More dolphins but not a sniff of fish. Lost my tackle just to rub my nose in it.

Starfire still following us. Yes we had managed to overtake them. We heard them on their VHF complaining to a fishing vessel to change course. A fat lot of good that will do. Slept better tonight after adding an extra blanket. It's getting much colder now and we are still on 35 degrees latitude which is level with Gibraltar.

20th May. Nice sunny day and wind predicted to drop. And it did so. Engine on to motor out of Azores High reading 1030 degrees. Unable to get weather download. Perhaps High is affecting Mailasail comms? Cockpit hood beginning to come apart but Stan is ready with the needle and cotton and spent a number of hours making a good job of an ever increasing lost cause. Stan is not happy with noisy engine. He has no time restraints and hates any level of noise. He was very adamant that he will get off in the Azores and join a boat less time restricted. I'm not sure he will be any better off as most boats these days rely on their engine to keep a reasonable pace going. 490 miles to go.

21st May Exactly one year since leaving the UK. I'm not celebrating until we actually get back. Not a good day. Engine has been running for 24 hours. And not much prospect of wind returning. Fingers crossed for Ernie and the engine mechanics. Cannot get weather report down load. Alan predicting 3 weeks on next passage which is 18 days longer than it should be. 370 miles to go.

22nd May. Engine on for second day. Complete flat calm and dolphins look so clear swimming alongside. A few turtles are also very visible. Starfire came alongside and we threw a line to them to enable a USB download of films as they had run out. Unfortunately Alan managed to collide and damage the Scarf.

6 hours later Starfire requested to came alongside again to get a copy of Alan's pictures of Starfire. Alan is a bit of a photographer and I must say his shots were very good. At the time I was below checking Ernie. As Starfire was also heading for The Azores and the damage previously done to DwW. I was not happy that Alan took an arbitory decision to agree without checking with me. I was not happy. I think he got the message. 250 miles to go.

23rd May. It's Jamie's birthday today. He's 28. Third day of motoring. At least motoring has enabled us to head further North to reach Horta. 5 days back we were on a heading further south to San Miguel because of our concern to stay below the troublesome LOWS.

This meant we had to contact Ian who was landing in Horta and would need to change his travel plans. How many times does this occur? Its unbelievable how crew arrangements always change.

Hamish fixed the Garmin GPS and the MARPA facility which was not reading correctly. He identified the problem of having to ensure the Nmeaa option was selected. He's a really good electronics and handy man. Engine still beavering away. It's done a great service but still 30 hours to go to Horta. Sat phone has run out of minutes. They really do get eaten up and very expensive but also very necessary.

24th May. Last few hours seem to drag on. However if I had been offered 14 days passage to The Azores I would have grabbed it. Alan pushing engine too hard. Well it's not his boat is it? I wonder how delivery boats are cared for on long passages without the owner on board. I also had a quiet word in his ear about the difference between professional crew and amateurs. Alan was very good at teaching but during stressful times of high winds he tended to get short tempered with crew not responding to helmsmen's orders. I said he should be more forgiving especially with Stan to whom he was being rather harsh. We Arrived Horta 20.30 hours with a lovely view of Pico Volcano. We managed to get a late meal in the famous Pete's Sports Bar. Fabulous atmosphere with lots of sailors and crew gathering together from all over the world. It reminded me of the scene in Star wars where they land on this planet in the middle of the universe. The Bar was full of visitors from all corners of the Universe which created a fantastic atmosphere of adventure exchanging stories of wondrous experiences.

25th May. It's Sunday and all shops closed as it's a Bank Holiday. Hoisted up mast to check rigging but forgot to take photos of Tri colour lamp so I would know what to replace back in the UK. Pleased with having made the trip up to the top without too much fear. Ian joined us last night and Hamish has left for his flight back to the UK.
Stan unable to find a boat needing crew and not using engine so looks like he will stay with us for the last leg to UK. Second meal in Pete's bar. There's a distinct lack of restaurants here. Strangely enough everyone

speaks passable English which is odd for a Portuguese Island. I think it's due to the fact that The Azores has been a longstanding whaling centre which attracted many traders and whaling boats from both England and the USA. Consequently the English language is widely taught and used.

26th May. Completed shopping for last leg and bought some spares from the Chandlery. Including a Reids Almanac for 60 Euros. Food and other things very cheap. Managed to get a run up to top of Caldero which had a lovely view over a sunken volcano which the youngest volcano was erupting approximately 50 years ago. It was a bit early in the year for the flowers and fauna to blossom but I got the feeling these islands would be beautiful in the summer, nevertheless still very green and verdant with superb views.
These islands were once THE Place for Whaling and one could still see the old harbour and whaling factories. I tried to buy an English version of Baliae by the author Crabtree (not sure what he's doing in the Azores as I read him as the coarse fisherman in England) but they didn't have any in stock. Pete's son gave me a couple of web addresses I could contact in the UK to obtain a copy. Pete's son now runs the Bar and the museum on the first floor. It contains loads of whale bones beautifully sculptured. They are called scrimshaws. The life in those times must have been very hard because the boats were very basic and the whales would normally be at least 20 miles off shore. Any slight misjudgement by the spearman could result in a capsize and the sea was not a friendly place here abouts. The island had various lookouts on strategically placed hilltops and each day a man would

keep watch and set off a rocket if he spotted a whales spout miles out to sea. He would shout Baleia on the phone. Then the whole town would spring into action and within a few minutes boats were launched and on their way to the hunt.

I'm so glad it's not practised anymore.

Our planned trip to Terciera is abandoned due to unfavourable wind. That's sailing.

27th May. Fuelled up and cleared out with customs after much messing around. Stan finally managed to paint our Logo on the harbour wall. This is a long standing tradition in Horta with thousands of paintings lining the wall. Due to clearing out problem I didn't get a chance to take photo but Ian did. It was a priority that I had one picture of Stan's good artistry. Perhaps he will see it again in 2011?

Departed from Horta and sailed between San Jorge, Terciera and Graciosa. Shame there's low cloud around as we leave this beautiful, peaceful place. 1200 miles to England. Hoping for a 10 day passage if winds favourable.

28th May. Ian had a difficult shift with night watch as he wasn't yet 100% with sail plan and the usual 35 knot gust caught him out. Making very good progress but very rolly and difficult to cook meals. Had to tighten band on Larry steering. He's is struggling a bit.

Have the feeling that crew now keen to get to destination with Falmouth looking favourite.

29th May. Not much happening which is good news for me. Changed gas bottle and discovered the tube wasn't secure with its jubilee clip. Alan was not happy as this could have been a major problem with leaking gas. One thing that will sink a boat is a fire so I was could see his concern. Bottle didn't last long. Not down to leaking gas I might add. I remember the Bosun in Jome marina; Tortola had a flea in his ear about refilling gas bottles. He said then he wasn't happy because he didn't have the right equipment and they were no longer doing refills. I think he only half filled them but still managed to charge me full whack. Just glad I bought a full bottle in Horta. Managed to get some reasonable sleep this night so feeling much better.

30th May. Larry not happy. Batteries not getting enough power. Could be that our 5 knots of speed is very border line for adequate power supply through Doris, the towed generator. 750 miles remaining to Falmouth and 1000 miles to Shoreham by sea.

31st May. Lack of wind so Engine on. But only 750 miles to Falmouth so adequate fuel on board to motor all the way if we have to. Wondered what the crew were thinking after 4 weeks passage making and 3000 miles covered. Alan was getting very impatient and taking it out of Stan. Stan wasn't complaining about criticism (What a fine fellow he is), but I felt Ian was not happy with Alan's bossing attitude.
Larry finally gave up the ghost which meant we would have to helm all night for the remaining 570 miles. Well done Larry for hanging on in there.

Weather looking good for remainder of passage.

1st June Cold and wet today and beginning to feel a bit homesick for Shoreham. No activity to speak of on board – good. Tried changing belt on Larry but its more serious so finally gave up on him. Running low on food but still plenty of canned stuff remaining from the original ARC provisioning. Tried to contact Northern Child on the SSB as we had arranged in Horta, but no joy. Alan reckons my PC software is demo only so fax downloads have no chance of getting through.

Reading Robin Knox Johnson autobiography of his 1963 passage single-handed round the world. And I think I have had it tough! Have lots of synergy with his exploits. I have a much better equipped boat but he didn't have crew concerns. Tomorrow we put DwW closer to England than she has been for 12 months. It rather cheered me up. 500 miles to Falmouth.

2nd June. We saw Dolphins which are much bigger than the usual porpoises. The Dolphins have a different swim pattern with circles rather than following the boat. Magnificent jumps high out of the water. I'm sure they were showing off. Feeling very hung over. Don't know why. It's extremely rolly and the bruises are numerous.

Doris is discharging electricity but batteries are getting drained. It must be the solar panel regulator is telling something different. It's very cold, wet and miserable. Well we are getting close to England. Absolutely no luck with fishing and managed to lose another lure today.

3rd June. Woke up in a foul mood which is very uncharacteristic for me. Felt tired and dirty and the bad weather didn't help. But remembered Robin's journey and poked myself to get out of being in such a silly mood. The gale passed over and the warm returned and we were 280 miles off Falmouth.

4th June. Engine on all day. Wind dropped and now only 200 miles remaining. Looking forward to seeing land. Funny how one is less fussy on the boat. Today I tried porridge for the first time since I was a youngster. With a dollop of blackberry jam it was rather nice. Checked engine with revs at 2300/2500 revs and appears to be ok. Never really got to grips with what are the perfect cruising revs for a 28 hp engine.

5th June. 60 miles left. It's difficult to comprehend that I have completed 10,000 miles.
Sighted Lands End first and arrived in Falmouth at 21.00 hours. In pub by 21.30 supping a pint of lager.
It feels completely alien with English speaking people. Now I am here I want to return to the Caribbean. What fickle beings us humans are. Had only a few beers and a whisky to celebrate our return to England. We were rafted up to another boat and I managed to fall off the boat next door. Couldn't explain to the others for my unbalanced state. I certainly didn't feel drunk. Perhaps I was subconsciously letting go after completing such a personal challenge.

I thought I would look forward to the rest of the passage back to Shoreham with easy night stops hopping back. Yet somehow it doesn't seem attractive anymore after all the adventures abroad.
Perhaps finally I have come to terms with the boat breaking down but CAN be repaired. I could now finally enjoy being skipper and owner. Especially after successfully completing the seventh step to heaven and the long trip back.

6th June. Chill out day in Falmouth. Ian knows the town very well since his son attended college here. He took us to a Cornish pasty café. Very tasty. Visited Museum and ended up with big hangover. Must be down to absence of alcohol for 10 days at sea.

7th June. Alan has left the boat to return to Portsmouth and his next assignment. We depart for Weymouth but come up against 47 knot winds. I wanted to carry on but crew didn't agree so we cut short and headed into Plymouth. I'm glad we did because the weather deteriorated. Despite a short day at sea we arrived in Mayflower marina very knackered indeed. It was very strange coming back here after exactly 53 weeks since joining the Portugal rally. It's a small world.

8th June. Dried out our wet clothes and had a very nice lunch in the Jolly Roger restaurant, before leaving for Portland, Unlike the year before, I was now confident enough to take DwW through the channel bypassing the trip around Drakes Island. There was plenty of room and plenty of depth. . Before long the wind dropped and we switched on the engine. Then changed our plans to visit Portland and carried on to Poole/IOW. The tide was against us for the Solent approach so we headed for Swanage and anchored just off the pier for a few hours rest awaiting a good tide. Ian got the fishing line out and believe it or not he caught a fish. The first one after 4000 miles.

9th June. Lovely sunny day. Took pictures of Harry's rock and The Needles. Two Volvo racing boats out practising. They certainly look the part for racing around the world. I thought of Pam and her adventure on one of the Clipper race boats. Especially her story of sailing for 6 weeks into a heading wind on the Indian Ocean leg.

Arrived in Cowes in a strengthening wind. Tied up and Ian cooked a nice curry. Met a guy in pub who said he had a boat in Antigua that he bought for £8000 and renovated himself. Nice if one has the time and skills.

Read the last of Robin Knox Johnson's exploits. What an extraordinary guy, what an improviser.

10th June. Last leg to Shoreham. Decided to motor through The Owers instead of going around the long way which would have been difficult in a 35 knot NE wind on the nose.

Just managed to sneak through the channel with 2 and half knots of tide against us. Coastguard continues to forecast strong winds rather than gale force conditions. It's now exceeding 40 knots. Back to good old Blighty. Rain, cold and gale force winds.

Finally the Shoreham power station tower came into view. I had dreamt of this moment for a number of months and now it was here. I wonder how I will adjust and move forward with my life.

The whole adventure had lasted almost 3 years and 12, 000 miles. My dream completed without major incident.

Epilogue

Many of the crew, friends and family asked me how I would feel when I returned to the UK. How would I settle down to a life of predictable activity, routine and security?

It was the 64,000 dollar question. Knowing myself I was fairly certain that I would not "go bananas", commit suicide or go off the rails with another woman or something so drastic. How long would it take me to re-adjust? That question was a bit closer to home. My previous visits back to the UK gave me some inkling. For instance I didn't want to listen to any news on the television. It was all so mundane and blown out of proportion by the media. It also seemed so irrelevant. I couldn't get into any sort of routine that Diane had, and I couldn't motivate myself to do anything around the house. Thankfully the weather was getting warmer and it helped me to adjust better. Also the family and friends bought me back down to earth.

Diane had arranged a welcome home gathering in a lovely hotel, which helped.

Gradually I began to get back into things. I organised a 10 day trip to the Channel Islands in early August. Which left me little time to complete all the jobs on the boat before we left. The jobs were not small. Antifouling the bottom. It was smothered in barnacles. Re-gluing and/or replacing most of the interior lining. Plus a dozen smaller jobs with the electronics. Larry repair would take a bit longer as it needed a major upgrade.

We set off for Cherbourg in a strong SW wind on the nose. After 8 hours of attempting to get round The Outer Owers I told the crew we would be out at sea all night just to get to Portsmouth let alone Cherbourg. We turned the boat around and headed back for Shoreham. It was a marked moment in my return to the UK. I was so fed up with the cold and the weather I said to the crew I was not setting sail the next morning. I was going to sell the boat. I couldn't quite grasp why I was so low. Well the next day was lovely and sunny with a favourable wind for Cherbourg. My previous night's thoughts were now just a memory. I think I had tried to re-enact days in the Caribbean and it just wasn't to be.

It's now December 2010 and with a long spell of not sailing the enthusiasm to get out on the water is getting very strong.

I am now in Australia and have just crossed Sydney harbour on the ferry. To our starboard are two Volvo racing boats battling it out with a brisk SW wind. They are superb boats and must be doing in excess of 15 knots with full sails up. I am very jealous and wish I was there. Perhaps they are getting ready for the Sydney Hobart Race on Boxing Day. Perhaps I could get a crew place.

Diane is very understanding.

What I would do next time

Buy a bigger boat at least 42 feet.

Buy a quicker boat and sacrifice a little bit of comfort and safety.

Set up the sails for traditional spinnaker or cruising shute rather than twin headsails

Make sure the gas supply is global compatible

Don't bother with mosquito netting unless going onto Pacific sailing

Be as careful as possible with crew selection. Try and qualify out any doubtful starters.Do not select any crew that you do not feel entirely happy with.

Do not spend your valuable budget on items that have not been proven to be necessary. There are lots and lots of good ideas and marketing persuasions to entice you to buy. Try and be very hard on purchase selection.

Yes a watermaker is a good buy. They still have some reliability issues but the advantages far outweigh this factor.

Overcome your fears and trepidations. Today boats are safe, secure and the technology around will guide you to your destination and fulfilment. Just make sure you prepare adequately and plan a passage to the maximum of safety within the data and information available especially the weather.